PRAISE FOR

HIRED: AN INSIDERS LOOK AT THE TRUMP VICTORY

"With his characteristic wit and take-no-prisoners style, Ted Malloch gives us the story of the 2016 election that the mainstream media all missed. Have fun!"

—F.H. BUCKLEY, AUTHOR OF *THE WAY BACK: RESTORING THE PROMISE OF AMERICA*

"Ted Malloch rode the inside track all the way to help Donald Trump achieve the 'presidency.' A descendant of President Theodore Roosevelt, Malloch helped set key themes for the Trump campaign and served as one of Trump's most stalwart supporters from the first days of Trump's candidacy."

—JEROME R. CORSI, PHD, NO. 1 *NEW YORK TIMES* BESTSELLING AUTHOR AND SENIOR STAFF WRITER WND

"Ted Malloch was the first writer to see and to understand Trump as the non-ideological, pragmatic, populist.Malloch makes clear why the America first spirit carried the day. Bravo!"

"All the way from Oxford Malloch saw what was coming—Brexit and Trumpism. This book tells the whole saga."

"An insider's guide to the greatest political achievement in American history. A must read."

"Malloch is a first person witness to the common sense conservatism that makes President Trump who he is and that will define his administration. Read this book by a first-class observer and part of his team."

HIRED

AN INSIDER'S LOOK *at* *the* TRUMP VICTORY

THEODORE ROOSEVELT MALLOCH

afterword by NIGEL FARAGE

WND Books

HIRED

Published by WND Books, Washington, D.C. WND Books is a registered trademark of WorldNetDaily.com, Inc. ("WND")

Book designed by Mark Karis

WND Books are available at special discounts for bulk purchases. WND Books also publishes books in electronic formats. For more information call (541) 474-1776, e-mail orders@wndbooks.com or visit www.wndbooks.com.

Paperback ISBN: 978-1-942475-47-7
eBook ISBN: 978-1-942475-46-0

Library of Congress Cataloging-in-Publication Data Available

Printed in the United States of America
17 18 19 20 21 22 LSI 9 8 7 6 5 4 3 2 1

To all the Deplorables, Irredeemables, and all the normal everyday, working people who had the good common sense to choose Donald J. Trump as their President

CONTENTS

PREFACE

EARLY IN THE MORNING OF NOVEMBER 9 the news stations announced that Donald Trump was the *president-elect.*

Taking 306 electoral college votes to Clinton's 232, Trump did what nearly every pundit, expert and pollster said was impossible: he won the US presidency.

Look at any election map and notice how red/Republican it is. Sweeping Florida, North Carolina, Ohio, and then quite unbelievably rust belt states, Pennsylvania, Michigan, and Wisconsin, Trump scored a knockout.

He won a landslide result and took the White House away from *both* Barrack Obama and his chosen Democrat heiress, the villainous, Hilary Clinton. She was expected to be coroneted and all the media, and all the celebrities, and all the inside political class were ready for Hilary to reign. They even built a gigantic stage for her in the shape of these United States in a huge civic center with a glass ceiling to celebrate the anticipated result.

But it was *not* meant to be.

Trump's unprecedented, and for many unexpected victory, came as a total *shock*. There was no way he could ever get to 270 we were repeatedly told. The polls had him down and the electoral map was difficult to worse. He simply would not, could not, win.

But Donald Trump prevailed. He never deterred from his simple and profound message: *To Make America Great Again*. And he had a straight flush—he ran the table and won a decisive victory carrying the House, the Senate, and governorships, just about everywhere. It was astounding and unpredicted.

His victory was that large, that monumental. It signaled realignment in politics and was part of a wave of nationalist-populist inspired efforts around the globe from Brexit to America and back again to Europe and elsewhere.

How did he do it? Why did it happen?

There were only a *very* few of us who believed from the start—who saw it as he saw it. I was with him from the moment he descended down the escalator in his gilted Trump Tower in New York City over a year and a half ago. He did not waver and neither did his stalwart and loyal supporters—which just grew and grew and mushroomed. They were evident in the large and excited rallies around the country he conducted and from all the media Trump collected. They grew through each decisive primary victory—where one by one—he knocked off every single Republican challenger, most of whom were experienced politicians.

In the general election there were bleak days and new challenges to face but the underreported support grew and grew, especially in the key battleground states. Like an iceberg it was just under the surface. It was evidenced in the forgotten people who had both rage and hope, who were "mad as hell and not going to take it anymore," while also plainly, wanting their country back.

Trump heard the *will of the people* and identified with them and was never fixed on the popular vote, realizing that the election demanded another kind of fixation. He tirelessly slugged through the three televised debates and traveled around all the key states so often he became well known. He spent less than his opponent and ran a most unconventional campaign.

He was after all a most unconventional candidate.

And the data shop secretly organized by his brilliant son-in-law supplied all the critical information to pinpoint the vote and micromanage the very directed effort. His astute communication director kept him on track and messaging while his vice presidential choice showed courage and humility in equal measure.

I have known Donald Trump for decades. He is an indefatigable person. He is strong and able. His Wharton financial education and years building a multi-billion dollar successful real-estate business make him a uniquely qualified person to actually run America: to be it's CEO.

I have known him from building golf courses in Scotland and hotels around the world but also seen his true heart. I have given to his various philanthropic causes in Florida and New York, played in his charity golf tournaments, and watched as he literally "gave back" to a country and the society he dearly loves. I joined the campaign early and worked with the nascent National Policy Council and gave strategies and policy advice on a host of issues. I appeared regularly in print from *Forbes* to *Breitbart* to WND and elsewhere and on air as a surrogate on CNN, FOX, SKY, and BBC and on the radio.

This is what deeply motivates Donald Trump: love of country.

He is a patriot first and foremost and he wants our country to restate those lasting and trusted values that have carried us this far. He wants everyone to prosper. Some make him out to be a narcissist or a bully. Nothing could be further from the truth.

Donald Trump is an authentic leader and a *doer* who will fix America, defend America, and make it safe and prosperous. He puts America first and his policies will do the same.

This is the story of *how and why* Donald Trump became president of these United States. They record my opinion about how this came to be and why this came to fruition at this particular juncture in time.

Let's start by looking then at why I supported Donald and what the case for Trump consisted of. We can then consider Trump's worldview and after inspect his opponent and her allies to see how seriously flawed they were. The context of this watershed election and the sense of nationalism, liberty, and populism make it a turning point in American, if not world history. But politics is also about policy and Trump's policies in the end won the day. In conclusion, we will see why he won and what it means for our Commercial Republic. At the end of the brutal election contest and into the first one hundred days for his Administration we will see the difference Trump can make and we will see Trump the builder at work.

But the best place to begin our back-looking glance of why and how Trump won such a resounding victory is to study the very Victory Speech he himself gave upon the announcement of his election to serve as America's forty-fifth president. Here is what he said that night:

Thank-you. Thank-you, very much, everyone. Sorry to keep
you waiting. Complicated business, complicated. Thank-you,
very much.

I've just received a call from Secretary Clinton. She
congratulated us. It's about us. On our victory, and I congratulated her and her family on a very, very hard-fought
campaign.

I mean, she fought very hard. Hillary has worked very
long and very hard over a long period of time, and we owe
her a major debt of gratitude for her service to our country.

I mean that very sincerely. Now it is time for America
to bind the wounds of division, have to get together. To all
Republicans and Democrats and independents across this
nation, I say it is time for us to come together as one united
people.

It is time. I pledge to every citizen of our land that I will
be president for all of Americans, and this is so important
to me. For those who have chosen not to support me in the
past, of which there were a few people, I'm reaching out to
you for your guidance and your help so that we can work
together and unify our great country. As I've said from the
beginning, ours was not a campaign but rather an incredible
and great movement, made up of millions of hard-working
men and women who love their country and want a better,
brighter future for themselves and for their family.

It is a movement comprised of Americans from all races,
religions, backgrounds, and beliefs, who want and expect our
government to serve the people, and serve the people it will.

Working together, we will begin the urgent task of
rebuilding our nation and renewing the American dream.

I've spent my entire life in business, looking at the untapped potential in projects and in people all over the world.

That is now what I want to do for our country. Tremendous potential. I've gotten to know our country so well. Tremendous potential. It is going to be a beautiful thing. Every single American will have the opportunity to realize his or her fullest potential. The forgotten men and women of our country will be forgotten no longer.

We are going to fix our inner cities and rebuild our highways, bridges, tunnels, airports, schools, hospitals. We're going to rebuild our infrastructure, which will become, by the way, second to none, and we will put millions of our people to work as we rebuild it. We will also finally take care of our great veterans who have been so loyal, and I've gotten to know so many over this eighteen-month journey.

The time I've spent with them during this campaign has been among my greatest honors.

Our veterans are incredible people. We will embark upon a project of national growth and renewal. I will harness the creative talents of our people, and we will call upon the best and brightest to leverage their tremendous talent for the benefit of all. It is going to happen. We have a great economic plan. We will double our growth and have the strongest economy anywhere in the world. At the same time, we will get along with all other nations willing to get along with us. We will be. We will have great relationships. We expect to have great, great relationships. No dream is too big, no challenge is too great. Nothing we want for our future is beyond our reach.

America will no longer settle for anything less than the

best. We must reclaim our country's destiny and dream big and bold and daring. We have to do that. We're going to dream of things for our country, and beautiful things and successful things once again.

I want to tell the world community that while we will always put America's interests first, we will deal fairly with everyone, with everyone.

All people and all other nations. We will seek common ground, not hostility; partnership, not conflict. And now I would like to take this moment to thank some of the people who really helped me with this, what they are calling tonight a very, very historic victory.

First, I want to thank my parents, who I know are looking down on me right now. Great people. I've learned so much from them. They were wonderful in every regard. Truly great parents. I also want to thank my sisters, Marianne and Elizabeth, who are here with us tonight. Where are they? They're here someplace. They're very shy, actually.

And my brother Robert, my great friend. Where is Robert? Where is Robert?

My brother Robert, and they should be on this stage, but that's okay. They're great.

And also my late brother Fred, great guy. Fantastic guy. Fantastic family. I was very lucky.

Great brothers, sisters, great, unbelievable parents. To Melania and Don and Ivanka and Eric and Tiffany and Barron, I love you and I thank you, and especially for putting up with all of those hours. This was tough.

This was tough. This political stuff is nasty, and it is tough. So I want to thank my family very much. Really fantastic. Thank you all. Thank you all. Lara, unbelievable job. Unbelievable. Vanessa, thank you. Thank you very much. What a great group.

You've all given me such incredible support, and I will tell you that we have a large group of people. You know, they kept saying we have a small staff. Not so small. Look at all of the people that we have. Look at all of these people.

And Kellyanne and Chris and Rudy and Steve and David. We have got tremendously talented people up here, and I want to tell you it's been very, very special.

I want to give a very special thanks to our former mayor, Rudy Giuliani. He's unbelievable. Unbelievable. He traveled with us and he went through meetings, and Rudy never changes. Where is Rudy. Where is he?

[Chanting "Rudy"]

Gov. Chris Christie, folks, was unbelievable. Thank you, Chris. The first man, first senator, first major, major politician—let me tell you, he is highly respected in Washington because he is as smart as you get. Sen. Jeff Sessions. Where is Jeff? A great man. Another great man, very tough competitor. He was not easy. He was not easy. Who is that? Is that the mayor that showed up? Is that Rudy?

Up here. Really a friend to me, but I'll tell you, I got to know him as a competitor because he was one of the folks that was negotiating to go against those Democrats, Dr. Ben Carson. Where's been? Where is Ben? By the way, Mike Huckabee is here someplace, and he is fantastic. Mike and his familiar bring Sarah, thank you very much. Gen. Mike Flynn. Where is Mike? And General Kellogg. We have over two hundred generals and admirals that have endorsed our campaign and there are special people.

We have twenty-two Congressional Medal of Honor people. A very special person who, believe me, I read reports that I wasn't getting along with him. I never had a bad second with him. He's an unbelievable star. He is—that's right, how did you possibly guess? Let me tell you about Reince. I've said Reince. I know it. I know it. Look at all of those people over there. I know it, Reince is a superstar. I said, they can't call you a superstar, Reince, unless we win it. Like Secretariat. He would not have that bust at the track at Belmont.

Reince is really a star and he is the hardest-working guy, and in a certain way I did this. Reince, come up here. Get over here, Reince.

Boy, oh, boy, oh, boy. It's about time you did this right. My god. Nah, come here. Say something.

[Reince Priebus: Ladies and gentlemen, the next president of the United States, Donald Trump! Thank you. It's been an honor. God bless. Thank God.]

Amazing guy. Our partnership with the RNC was so important to the success and what we've done, so I also have to say, I've gotten to know some incredible people.

The Secret Service people. They're tough and they're smart and they're sharp and I don't want to mess around with them, I can tell ya. And when I want to go and wave to a big group of people and they rip me down and put me back down in the seat, but they are fantastic people so I want to thank the Secret Service.

And law enforcement in New York City, they're here tonight. These are spectacular people, sometimes under appreciated unfortunately. We appreciate them. So it's been what they call an historic event, but to be really historic, we have to do a great job, and I promise you that I will not let you down. We will do a great job. We will do a great job. I look very much forward to being your president, and hopefully at the end of two years or three years or four years or maybe even eight years you will say so many of you worked so hard for us, with you. You will say that—you will say that that was something that you were—really were very proud to do and I can—thank you very much.

And I can only say that while the campaign is over, our work on this movement is now really just beginning. We're going to get to work immediately for the American people, and we're going to be doing a job that hopefully you will be so proud of your president. You will be so proud. Again, it's my honor.

It's an amazing evening. It's been an amazing two-year period, and I love this country. Thank-you.

Thank-you, very much. Thank-you to Mike Pence.

INTRODUCTION

THE NEW ROOSEVELT

Donald Trump is perhaps best viewed as the twenty-first century Theodore Roosevelt.

The two leaders have much in common—from style and swagger to substance and outlook. The last century would not have bent along the American arc were it not for our unexpected president and this century may not go our way without the likes of a Trump. There would be no Panama Canal, no national parks, no trust busting without Roosevelt. There will be no changes in Washington without the likes of a Trump.

On a hot summer August day, at the beginning of the twentieth century, Theodore Roosevelt gave his most famous "New Nationalism" speech in Kansas. He sounded much like the enthusiastic and charismatic candidate Donald Trump sounds today.

The speech centered on the uplift of humanity and our country, "this great republic" and its ultimate triumph. Such bold rhetoric was not thought audacious but rather inspiring. Trump's claim, "to make America great again," is nothing less.

THE VALUE OF CAPITAL AND LABOR

For Roosevelt the history of America had become the central feature in world history. He said that, "each of us stand erect, and should be proud that we belong, not to a dozen little squabbling contemptible commonwealths, but to the mightiest nation upon which the sun shines." He decried all factionalism and division. Trump is doing very much the same thing, calling all Americans—regardless of their station in life—to greatness. It is the combination of all our individual talents that makes this country great.

Echoing Lincoln, Roosevelt talked at length about the value of capital and of labor. His words included, "wise kindness and charity"—but not "to weaken our arm or numb our hearts." Trump has said more or less the same in language of our own times. He is a democratic capitalist and wants everyone to benefit from its riches. He, like Roosevelt, extols the strenuous life, a work ethic, and the virtues of spiritual capital.

Restoring America's main objectives in human betterment, measured in equality of opportunity, Roosevelt wanted America to strive again—to find its full glory. Trump realizes what we have lost in Obamanation and calls it the abomination that it is. The country wants to find its rightful place again and this is why Trump resonates, not just with Republicans but also with Reagan Democrats and even the trade unions. He resonates with every aspiring soul who wants the freedom to be what America always was—a beacon of hope and a land of opportunity.

A STRONG POLICY OF AMERICAN NATIONALISM

Based on a fair chance "to make of himself all that in him lies," Roosevelt's urge was one of true capacity building: personal and national. It was one that included a clause that every citizen should offer the commonwealth their highest service. Trump knows this from his own successful business career and all his commercial dealings and globetrotting. He also realizes that we have to stand up to our adversaries and contain the new evils that abound and threaten our very way of life.

Such a "square deal" freed all persons from "sinister influence or control of special interests." Calling for corporate responsibility, Roosevelt put forth a strong, effective policy of American Nationalism. He said, "No man should receive a dollar unless that dollar has been fairly earned." He wanted a sound financial system, an efficient army and navy, large enough to ensure our security and guarantee the peace. Trump is saying the same thing.

ANOTHER KIND OF CONSERVATION

Roosevelt sought a form of "conservation" in the original meaning of the term—for both natural resources and the country's moral foundations. Trump desires nothing less than to make America similarly strong again in word and deed. He too is a conservationist. He would confront our enemies and in the "art of the deal" reform trade and investment to favor America. He would no longer outsource our foreign policy to the Russian president Vladimir Putin. Nor would he outsource our manufacturing to China.

This spirit of "broad and far-reaching" nationalism meant for Roosevelt that we "work for our people as a whole."

Defending property as well as human welfare, Roosevelt sought material progress, technological advancement, and a nation of prosperity. All these lead to "the moral and national welfare of all good citizens." He saw America's place as leader of the twentieth century. He witnessed no class divide. Neither did he parse citizens by gender, race, or national origin. For him, there were no hyphenated Americans. The same rhetoric appears in the words of Trump in recent debates and on the campaign trail. He could unite America like no other candidate because, while an outsider politically, he is a truly national candidate who actually believes in America. His legal form of immigration would find support from Roosevelt. So too would his defense of our borders—the very borders Roosevelt fought for in the first place.

GOOD GOVERNMENT IS ROOTED IN GOOD CITIZENSHIP
When Roosevelt spoke, he stressed "good character"—character that makes a good person: a good spouse, a good worker, and a good neighbor. And he ended his speech with a clarion call (as was his entire two term Presidency) for good government rooted in good citizenship. Trump would do precisely the same. He would clean house, get rid of overregulation and fix both the tax code and the spirit of America. He would carry a big stick and he would make Congress work for the people, not special interests. He would end cronyism, as did Roosevelt first in the New York State assembly, and then in the civil service.

Trump is indeed the *new* Roosevelt. For America to survive and flourish we need his action and determinism, his enthusiasm and will to succeed.

1

THE CASE FOR TRUMP

THE MANHATTAN POPULIST

John Quincy Adams, quintessential Boston Brahman and arch-enemy of a General and bumpkin-turned-president Andrew Jackson, had a plan.

Rumors circulated that Jackson was illiterate (Adams had called him "a barbarian who could not write a sentence of grammar and hardly could spell his own name") and Adams amused himself with the thought of giving Jackson an *honorary* Harvard degree, the speech for which was traditionally given in Latin. So Adams arranged to have the backwoods president invited and assumed the illiterate Jackson would decline.

Jackson accepted.

On graduation day, the erudite Cambridge crowd swelled with western Massachusetts farmers. Adams and the Harvard trustees sat in the front very assured that Jackson would make a total jackass out of himself. The president took the stage, removed a dollar bill from his pocket, and read the words *E pluribus Unum* from the back. The crowd went wild with glee. Jackson went further: *E pluribus Unum*, my friends. *Sine qua non*. The speech was over, and Jackson had won. Again.

Whether the story is totally true or not doesn't matter. Jackson was the first celebrity President since George Washington because he knew how to best men like Adams. And Jackson knew Adams and the New England East Coast establishment thought he'd act like a jackass, and that's why Jackson made it the symbol of the new party he founded. What is less known is that Jackson the populist was also the champion of institutions and sound government.

Populists seek a protector of the faith, and the cornerstone of that faith is the American experiment.

Thus, populists seek those who share identification with institutions and a commitment to defend those institutions. Jackson's populist vision was founded on a strong nation wherein the primacy of institutions was all the detailed policy his constituents required of him.

The populism that Jackson tapped into would make him the first president elected inland from the eastern seaboard, and, in the minds of his constituents, the first president not elected by big cities and big plantations. For many, it heralded a fulfillment of the *anti-elite* republicanism on which they believed the country had itself been founded in its colonial revolt against unfair taxation without representation.

The salient combination of anti-elitism, continental nationalism, and Lord Protector of institutions has been revived at times, most recently by Donald Trump.

That he is wealthy is irrelevant—many populists, from

Jackson to progressive James Weaver—were wealthy. The key feature of these populists is that they appear concerned with America and *not* politics, which many cynical rural voters believe to be mutually exclusive. They are as populists, in many ways, anti-political.

This Jacksonian concern for America is a kind of nationalism and it was widely viewed as the antidote to the sectionalism that had pervaded presidential elections up until then.

Similarly, Trump's nationalism can be seen as a rebuke of Obama's tribalism, just as Jackson's election was a rebuke to Adams' and later Calhoun's sectionalism. And Trump's popularity is an affirmation that many believe that the country is stronger and better off with a decisive, unapologetically nationalist president.

Like Jackson, Trump is reflexively dismissive of overly detailed policy positions, which to populists are but smoke signals to the tribe that dissipate into thin air once the candidate is elected. Bernie Sanders is currently the tribesman most obviously consumed with sending up signals to call the progressive tribe together. But it is the bought-and-paid-for Hillary and the ideologically zealous who are the most devious tribalists in this race.

Populist nationalists wisely dismiss their smoke signals as political inventions that have no relationship to the reality of governing. These patriots see theirs as an establishment game not worth playing. For them the stakes are much higher—they are about *America First*.

It would be a mistake to project identity politics onto populists—as farmers or rednecks or nativists or immigrant factory workers or, as we hear it said today, angry white Americans.

Andrew Jackson's *E pluribus Unum* moment has become

populist lore, but it summarizes his entire platform: a strong, unified, republican America—which is a kind of country nationalism that Jefferson feared would be crushed by the disproportionate power of cities and their urban cabals.

Donald Trump recently said he could shoot someone on Fifth Avenue and not lose voters. He could have claimed that he could give a Harvard speech in three words—*E pluribus Unum*—and he would gain voters. And like Jackson, the establishment (even in his own party) would label him a jackass, and Trump would wear it as a badge of honor and win another election.

After *E pluribus Unum*, Andrew Jackson won 77 percent of the electoral votes in his bid for a second term in 1832. And in Jackson's farewell speech he delivered a lengthy, impassioned warning to the regular, everyday Americans—"the planter, the farmer, the mechanic, and the laborer"—that the establishment would use money and the media to undo his many accomplishments.

Trump has animated the nationalist spirit of Jackson from a glass and gold-plated Manhattan skyscraper, his own national Tower, and like a good populist, he probably doesn't even know it. Or does he?

THE APPRENTICE

We all watched the reality TV show *The Apprentice,* hosted by the real estate magnate and chairman of the board, now Republican presidential nominee, and the one and only, Donald J. Trump.

The show was a smash hit and ran for fourteen seasons on NBC to a *huge* (did I mention, it was *huge?*) audience.

It was billed as "the ultimate job interview." By process of elimination, one contestant was eliminated per episode—ending with Trump uttering the now-famous and memorable words: "You're fired!"

Suppose Trump decided to use this very same format, with the good Dr. Ben Carson as moderator, to interview and then select his vice presidential running mate, to join him on the Republican ticket this fall?

Now, we know the VP slot is not "worth a bucket of spit," as John Adams, first vice president of these United States, once stated. But someone has to attend all those funerals, cut the ribbons, and fly off to Des Moines when some tragedy strikes. Occasionally, the No. 2 even becomes No. 1, in the case of death. And a *good* choice can garner votes or balance a ticket.

Filmed live at Trump Tower in New York City, watch the vice presidential "Apprentice" show that will interview these ten finalists for the chance of a lifetime—to be literally "a heartbeat away" from the presidency.

And the contestants are:

JOHN KASICH OR MIKE PENCE, Republican governor of Ohio, age sixty-three, experience both as a state-level executive and in the House of Representatives, well-liked, clean hands, helped Trump win by staying in the race even though he did a deal with "Lucifer," Ted Cruz. He was rarely insulted by Trump, which is quite an accomplishment. He can deliver working-class and independent votes—and most important the critical battleground state of Ohio. An alternate would be Mike Pence the Governor of next door, Indiana.

Odds: good

MARCO RUBIO, Republican senator from Florida, age forty-four, Cuban, "Little Marco," was drubbed by Trump in the primaries and ridiculed, but he is not running for the Senate again. He has supposedly kissed and made up with Trump, but he did insult the size of his manhood, probably an unforgivable sin.

Odds: fair at best

NEWT GINGRICH, former Republican speaker of the House of Representatives, age seventy-two, author of the winning "Contract with America," is an inside-outsider. An early Trump booster and adviser, but the chances have been called a "moon shot." Such a self-promoter would possibly edge out The Donald himself. So while he is on a short list, his chances are slim to none.

Odds: long

SUSANA MARTINEZ, Republican governor of New Mexico, age 56, she endorsed Rubio, a no-no, but is chairwoman of the all-powerful Republican Governors Association. She has also

criticized Trump on Mexican immigrants but is two very valuable things: Hispanic! And a woman!
Odds: fair

CHRIS CHRISTIE, Republican governor of New Jersey, age
fifty-three. The rough and tumble Newark native, is a bully and
a street fighter. As a Bruce Springsteen fan and the first rival
to support Donald Trump, he has become a *very* loyal follower
and is a surrogate speaker for Trump already. He appears most
willing—perhaps too eager?
Odds: fair

CONDOLEEZA RICE, former Bush secretary of state and
national security expert, now provost at Stanford University,
age sixty-one. African-American woman with a doctorate in
Kremlinology, talented beyond compare, certainly a good
counterweight to Hillary but evidences no interest in electoral
politics. Would be a good "secretary of offense," if Trump were
to initiate such a role.
Odds: long

ARNOLD SCHWARZENEGGER, former Republican governor
of California, age sixty-eight. A reality TV type and muscle man
himself, Donald picked him to replace his character on "The
Apprentice" this season. But there is so much baggage in his
closet, and he is not a real conservative. His WWF fans would
like, it but after the sordid affair with his maid he would not
play very well for the woman vote. And Trump already has the
biker vote wrapped up.
Odds: very long

DICK CHENEY, former Bush 43 VP, neo-conservative, age seventy-five, very bad heart and bad shot, knows the ropes very well and was in effect COO, running the whole show for Bush the Younger. He announced his support for Trump last week, one of the only party elders to do so. Trump was likely wise not to put him in charge of the selection process this time around or he would choose himself.

Odds: very long

SARAH PALIN, former Republican governor of Alaska and huge tea party supporter, had her own reality TV show, aged fifty-two. Came out early swinging for Trump when he needed it most. As the VP choice of John McCain's losing effort to Obama, she has been there and took the heat. It would be hard to put lipstick on her, though.

Odds: moderate

THEODORE ROOSEVELT MALLOCH, Republican *extraordinaire*, Oxford professor, Ph.D., best-selling author, earliest Trump supporter (see: WND archive), international political economist of some renown, accomplished corporate strategist, served on dozens of boards, held ambassadorial position for President Reagan in the United Nations (UN), worked in the State Department and in the US Senate. No skeletons, great namesake and very good-looking.

Odds: out of the park

AND THE WINNER IS?
You guessed it ...

FOR *NOT* AGAINST TRUMP

Most of us on the right were hardly surprised by the *National Review* (*NR*) piece this week. Many of these tired, old voices, and people like George Will, who have the most to lose in a Trump victory, have already been chiming away in unison on all the pundit mainstream talk shows.

It is essentially a *last ditch* effort to try and stop the inevitable. In actuality, by mounting this foolish and vitriolic effort, they have probably handed Trump the fastest route to the Presidency and will increase his poll standings by more than 10 percent. *National Review* is truth be told, not what it used to be! Its' readership has dwindled and its editor sure *ain't* no Bill Buckley, in any way, shape or form.

I am a 'movement' conservative. I attended an evangelical college, did a doctorate under Straussians and Voeglinians, and have been active in dozens of conservative causes, policies, and think tanks. I was at an early age a foot soldier in the State Department under President Reagan, worked for Republican Senators Trible, Lugar and Dole, in the Senate, and was appointed by Reagan and served under Bush 41 in a high ranking UN post. My books have been on global strategy, international economics, and more recently, practical wisdom in management, the virtues, spiritual capital, and generosity. I do political economy or PPE, as the Brits call it. I know conservatism from the top to bottom.

The reason the *NR* crew dislikes Trump is because he is a *doer*—not an idle thinker or theorist, as are they. He represents a kind of national conservatism that has a popular rather than an elitist stance. But to the point, if he wins, *they loose.*

If you look at the list of writers in the *NR* issue, "Against Trump," they all back Cruz, Rubio, and Bush. Their candidates have *lost*—or will, and they are left backing the wrong horse. *NR* has, unfortunately, as has the *Weekly Standard,* become the GOE, establishment rags that no longer represent either real conservatism or the evolving GOP. They are that insignificant.

The motivation for the *NR* ilk simply put is: *life or death.* They want their cushy jobs, going on talk shows, getting free lunches and cocktails, being important and the prestige it brings. They are part of the 'ruling political class' and that will end. Their *salons* and gravy train will cease and they will be on the out rather than on the inside.

The myth of this crowd is that they accomplish things. Largely, they have not, unless you count earning fat paychecks and wider waistlines as accomplishments. I suppose they could all write books no one will read or just be bitter.

The *NR* effect on the election in my estimation is negligible. It is a 'news cycle' story. Trump is on a roll and will clean the table. This nomination will be all over in six weeks, which is *why* they are so desperate, right now. This helps Donald Trump, as everyday Americans, the real voters, are sick and tired of the punditry and the name-calling and the deceit by these characters.

Don't worry, conservatism is in good hands. Look at the growing number of real conservatives backing Trump: Dan Oliver, who was on the *NR* board and best friend to Bill Buckley, Conrad Black, Larry Kudlow, Laura Ingraham, Danillo Petranovich (who wrote Bill Buckley's last book with him), Nic Capaldi, the Catholic libertarian, more and more elected officials, Sarah Palin the latest, and the list goes on and on… It will only grow. Senator Jeff Sessions will be the *next to* endorse Trump. I should also say, Trump also has a lean but brilliant campaign staff. General Sam Clovis, directs policy, Corey Lewandowski is a brilliant strategist, who keeps things running, Hope Hicks, is both gorgeous and a PR wiz, and his spokesperson, Katrina Pierson, is as articulate as they come. All are *real* and tested conservatives.

In many ways this old conservative establishment has lost touch—as they are *both* removed from the travail and demands of everyday life, from economic anxiety experienced by the middle class, and they do not live in the flyover zone. They are *captives* of Washington, DC, a one-factory town, and its insidious culture and have become complete insiders, complicit in the malaise of current governing. They *go along* to *get along*. They are, in fact, part of the problem and they all fear Trump will excise them—and he will.

Trump's nomination is no longer an *if. Nearly all* of the *NR* twenty-two will, in time, back or vote for Trump. They have *no* alternative. Hillary is an option, seriously? I personally doubt she will be the Democrat candidate anyway, after she is indicted. Much as Trump might like to run against her, the likelihood is fading by the day.

If history is any lesson, and conservatives generally believe it is, then just like the Bush crowd lost out to Reagan in the 1980 primaries, they all came around and backed the Gipper. Reagan even made Bush (who he disliked) vice president and allowed the competent Jim Baker, to be his chief of staff in the White House. It was big of him. Which job do you want Ted Cruz? Secretary of homeland security? Or how about, chief "Apprentice" wall builder? Rubio would be a good cabinet choice, too, or a do nothing VP. Bush could be ambassador to free Iraq, since that has worked out so well for his family. Watch and see it all unfold in the *next* six months. You heard it here, first.

NR won't go out of business; it is barely in business now. It looses money and with this electioneering gimmick, its charitable tax-free status could be in jeopardy. *NR's* circulation has in fact fallen like a stone. The market forces (honestly, for all magazines) and stale editorial have brought it to where it is.

Buckley himself would hardly recognize his old rag. Make no mistake, we sorely need another Buckley, a *very* rare breed, a razor wit, and—another debate show as good as "Firing Line." Rich Lowry could never pull that off. He is so boring and less than captivating in person. Buckley would have eaten him for lunch. Maybe he could have sharpened his ever-present pencils?

The conservative movement is *strong*, stronger than ever. Conservatism is after all a so-called, 'big tent' and Trump knows that and can also appeal to many Democrat voters, the unions, blacks, legal immigrants, and the young. His rallies are over the top and represent all elements of the conservative tradition. There are, I remind you, *four* types of conservative disposition: natural rights conservatives, pure traditionalists, neocons, and radical Catholics. Libertarians often have conservative 'streaks' but are essentially anarchists, as Hayek himself disclosed.

Trump crosses all these and is an "America First," free-market, low-tax, pro-growth conservative. But in essence he is still an *entrepreneur*. He gets things done, understands profit and loss, and will both balance the budget and curtail our debt, while bringing America back. The pendulum is *swinging*—you can see it. It is palpable.

There are *amazing* similarities between Trump and Teddy

Roosevelt. And TR ended up on Mount Rushmore. We better get some more rock—as Trump could do the same by restoring America's greatness.

HOW TO HIRE A CEO OF THESE UNITED STATES

The US economy is in a shambles. There is little to no growth; our trade deficit with other countries balloons; and we are *not* creating enough decent jobs.

In fact, our job creation is pathetic. Last month the economy added only thirty-eight thousand new jobs—the *worst* number since 2010.

The unemployment number says 4.7 percent, but the *real* number is at least double that. Some claim it totals over 93 million people!

The participation rate is a better account—it measures more than those who have looked for a job in just the last four weeks. Increasingly, Americans are giving up and stop looking for work—and good jobs, that pay high wages, are even rarer to come by.

The chief economist for the National Association of Credit Unions called the US economic outlook "gloomy" and said there is "no silver lining" looking immediately ahead.

Our wage growth has been nonexistent for more than a decade now. As Capital Economics put it, "the weakness in payrolls is widespread."

And who is to blame for this? President Obama—along with his inept team who have failed to perform. He should stop all the chest thumping and globetrotting and go back to school. Private forecasters estimate that US economic growth is running a meager 2 percent or less, down from a paltry 2.4 percent expansion over the past two years. This is plain unacceptable! We need a president who can realize 4 or 5 percent growth rates.

The US economy frankly has failed to regain momentum. Some smart people are arguing we are in for years of "stagnation or stagflation," with lower standards of living and an erosion of wealth for the middle class, which means little economic equality. And that doesn't even admit to the risk of another recession looming on the horizon. What are Americans to do?

What we need is a new CEO. We should as an electorate use proven search techniques to find the *next* president.

If we did this the way a big company does it, we would hire a qualified executive search firm, the likes of Korn Ferry or another, to find us the *best* and *most qualified* person for the position.

And what would that search firm look for?

The job description they would follow would not be proscribed by the political parties or the media but dictated by the dire conditions we face.

America needs to find a vibrant, new CEO to address the personal, strategic and organizational drivers affecting its dynamics and performance. And, as noted, that performance has been worse than poor.

We need to achieve alignment on strategic direction and risk, secure the best people for the right executive roles (the cabinet) and build the capabilities necessary to deliver superior performance.

Only this kind of focus will create good new jobs and deliver wealth for the country over the longer term.

The research indicates that there are three key elements that influence CEO effectiveness (and we need them in the next president): Focus, Dynamism, and Strategy.

If we used a science-based assessment that predicts fit, the United States could accelerate the development of needed capabilities and improve the effectiveness of government. It could also demonstrably turn the economy around.

Truthfully, we likely need less government, less funding, not more, along with old-fashion *excellence* in government, the likes of which the private sector enjoys.

By optimizing overall effectiveness, a strong CEO as president could optimize effectiveness, impact, and legacy. Optimizing performance through team composition, diversity of skill and talent, team dynamics and management processes, the next president needs to be a doer, not a politician who uses inflamed ideology or false ego to impede progress. He needs to be achievement-oriented not a legislative game-player or a tinhorn.

Using rigorous, research-based methods, a new Cabinet, as a coordinated executive team, should devise and articulate a clear, ambitious and compelling purpose, direction and business model for the country: a contract for growth.

The president should align roles with business-oriented strategies and operating structures. By assessing and properly planning for risk tolerance, the president could then be bold and forthright. Within one hundred days, the president could begin to turn the economy back toward growth with the right policies and initiatives.

By enabling significant structural change (such as lower personal and corporate taxes, curtailment of limiting or duplicative regulation and movement to a balanced budget) and rapid, confident decision-making, a president, operating like a CEO, could navigate toward more effective governance. They could, working with Congress, in a word, get things done.

Putting the right people in the right positions and perfecting their management routines will make government both more appropriate and efficient. We need to stop doing many things, deregulate others, streamline still other processes, and focus on one big thing: *creating good jobs by growing the economic pie for all.*

It is the president's task to synchronize vision, mission, and goals to ensure everyone is pulling in the same direction.

Picture a perfectly aligned crew that rows together. That kind of supreme effort, that kind of expert skill and that kind of motivation is what the country urgently needs in 2016.

And only an experienced business leader who has done it is up to the demanding, even daunting task.

We don't need another politician of any ilk—left or right— we need something *different* this time around. Why? Because the stakes are so high and America has only one chance to stage a comeback, to be robust again.

We need a CEO to run the United States to work to create all these good jobs. It's about jobs, stupid!

Donald Trump, *you're hired!*

THE NOBLE TRUMP

One can say of Donald Trump what Menenius says of Coriolanus, in Scene 1 of Shakespeare's play "Coriolanus":

"His heart's his mouth."

In fact, Menenius prefaces this with these lines:

His nature is too noble for this world:

He would not flatter Neptune for his trident,

Or Jove for's power to thunder.

Here's a translation for those of you who need one: He won't kowtow to the powers that be but will speak his mind, even if it gets him in trouble or held in disregard.

That used to be called honesty, but in an age of baby talk, political correctness and mostly bulls--t, I guess it can at times look like dishonesty. It is perhaps Orwellian that Trump's truth is at times taken as the opposite.

For Trump is honest beyond all normalcies; at least in the sense in which Obama's/Hillary's Washington culture of deceit and falsehoods has come to define the new norm.

Trump can't help but call it like he sees it. He is not the typical economist or academic pundit, describing things on one hand and then on the other, to make a debating point or cover his a--.

Neither is he the archetypical Democratic politician, constantly lying between his teeth, always telling people what they want to hear.

Rather, Trump embodies the case of an upfront businessman who tells it like it is, cuts an honest and honorable deal, and then upholds his word in a bond of both legal contractual substance and of philosophical pragmatism. He keeps his word.

His goal, after all, is to get things done and to do what works. He does not have some huge inherited ideological agenda, and he is most certainly not wedded to either the failed neo-conservatism of military intervention or the problematic socialist rhetoric of redistribution. Instead, flexibility is his mantra.

Whether Trump "is too noble for this world" I don't know. Maybe he's just fed up with the phony political elites on both sides of the aisle who are selling out our country to foreigners for their own personal power and gain. Maybe he is so outside the present, corrupt, and corrupting system that he is able to stand back and name it for what it is.

Let's think about this old-fashioned word, noble, for a minute, for it seems to have exited our everyday lexicon. In the knights of yore, nobility was lauded and held in highest esteem.

We rarely hear it used today, certainly in the field of political behavior. Defined as having or sharing the true qualities of high moral purpose, being noble had synonyms like honorable, upright, decent, worthy, uncorrupted, ethical, reputable, brave, unselfish and magnanimous? These were virtues of excellence.

Noble purpose was best seen as a statement of your true calling in life and especially in the work you do. It was called a vocation.

This differentiated you from others and inspired you, and those around you, to succeed while honoring your core values.

Purpose is becoming all the rage today in companies and organizations because it links work to meaning. We all want meaningful lives, lives that matter. Beyond profit, which is short term in motivation, noble purpose makes for a greater cause—more enduring and tied to a telos (an end) that benefits all, toward some common good.

This nobility is something that can leverage natural needs creating high-level thinking and actions that are tied to a lasting worldview. Noble ideas, you realize, build cultures that form institutions that shape the world.

What is your noble purpose?

Here is the one that motivates Donald Trump and his game plan as a future president of the United States and leader of the entire free world.

First, his jumping off point for a noble purpose and a related strategy cascades at every level and every policy he articulates. That point is a simple phrase and his tagline, namely, To Make American Great Again (MAGA). America comes first.

Second, proving this noble way, Trump has a distinctive narrative. He has codified his impact on all of American society. He personalizes his inclusive message to explain what matters and what does not. He is dead serious about his intentions and his plan to enact MAGA. For him our future and that of our larger civilization depend on nothing less.

Third, Trump is winning hearts and minds by launching and activating his noble purpose. His repeated message and candidacy is aspirational. He plans to accelerate it with wins that change the entire process of politics and the landscape of Washington culture. Donald Trump, if anything, is a doer—he is applied. He is no ideologue or pontificator. He will deliver.

Fourth, Trump uses visuals and real stories to make his point. He is alive, real and compelling, as no other voice in this election year. His message is external and has gone viral. Trump's noble purpose is aligned with what he says he will do. Trump, in a word, will execute. What he promises will become manifest.

Make no mistake: Trump is embedding his noble purpose and creating a larger system that can live on and on. Both voters and history itself will, of course, judge his performance.

He relishes this as someone who has carried a Profit & Loss and a Balance Sheet mentality in the world of fierce business. MAGA, like Reagan's Morning in America, or JFK's, New Frontier, or TR's, Square Deal, can live on, transforming our country and the world for this twenty-first century.

It is a noble purpose, and Trump is its unique and timely messenger. Trump is not a typical self-serving politician. He is an authentic leader.

Sir John Templeton, the greatest investor of the last century and a mentor of mine, believed that awareness that one's life can reflect a sense of higher purpose no matter what the circumstances changes life. He thought that humans in many cultures and historical epochs have pursued noble purposes by answering God's call as each hears it.

You see, noble purpose can be pursued both in heroic acts and in everyday behavior. Ordinary people—teachers, business professionals, workers, parents, and citizens—can also ennoble what they do by being mindful of its deepest meaning.

Purpose brings coherence and satisfaction to people's lives, producing joy in good times and resilience in hard times. It also presents a paradox: Hard work in service of noble purpose that transcends personal gain is a surer path to happiness than the self-indulgent pursuit of material things for their own sake.

The closer we come to God's purpose for us, the more satisfied our lives become. Trump realizes this and is himself sacrificing to return America to its original path.

His noble purpose is identical to that of the Founders who

used the famous line in their first declaration, signaling what America was all about: life, liberty and the pursuit of happiness, understood not as some hedonistic satisfaction but as *eudemonia*.

2

TRUMP'S WORLDVIEW

COMMONSENSE CONSERVATISM—

FROM REAGAN TO TRUMP

The best spokesperson for common sense in recent times was Ronald Reagan.

In his farewell address, the fortieth president defined his revolution as "a rediscovery of our values and our common sense."

Actually, from the very start of his political career, Reagan attributed his success to his belief in the idea that government "could be operated efficiently by using the same common sense practiced in our everyday life, in our homes, in business and private affairs."

Today presidential candidate Donald Trump, taking up Reagan's mantle, has laid claim to the phrase "commonsense conservatism." What exactly does this mean?

COMMON SENSE AND PRUDENCE

In economics, commonsense behavior can be seen as "risk aversion," defined as a predilection to take precautionary moves, especially when an uncertain future is seen as perilous, full of risks that can neither be fully calculated nor avoided.

In accounting, "risk aversion," a fundamental concept, is defined as prudence, a standard used to determine, for instance, the time when revenue can and should be recognized—a calculation that typically is neither unimportant nor inconsequential.

Lawyers still abide by the so-called prudent (man) judgment rule to argue cases at law involving judgments of right and wrong.

The Catechism of the Catholic Church, in Part Three, Section One, Chapter One, Article 7, identifies the "human virtues," with an addition written in 1806 devoted to articulating the "cardinal virtues" by quoting St. Thomas Aquinas in reference to prudence.

That text reads: "Prudence is the virtue that disposes practical reason to discern our true good in every circumstance and to choose the right means of achieving it." It went on to conclude with some sound advice, namely: "The prudent man looks where he is going."

If prudent behavior is right reason in action, then why has the importance of prudence to common sense been mostly abandoned, forfeited in more recent times and nearly totally forgotten by our post-modern culture and governments?

RESURRECTING COMMON SENSE

Let's trace the history of common sense's demise, for in so doing we will then be able to suggest ways for its possible resurrection.

For Aristotle any conception of the "good life" employed practical wisdom.

Knowledge of the good life is what elevated prudence into a virtue in the first place and identified it as wisdom. This "practical wisdom" for Aristotle was rooted in our experience. Experience teaches us how to apply universal principles to the particular circumstances of life. Aristotle's inquiry of "practical wisdom" and the "good life" was meant to inform human action.

In the "Nicomachean Ethics," Aristotle wrote: "Prudence is that virtue of the understanding which enables men to come to wise decisions about the relation to happiness of the goods and evils."

By the time of English political philosopher Thomas Hobbes, however, at the start of the modern era, we witness a complete rejection of such thinking.

Hobbes finds prudence no longer to be a proper concept in philosophy. He cast it aside as "mere conjecture." This turned classical ethics on its head as prudence was no longer a virtue at all.

During the Scottish Enlightenment, Adam Smith (who was first and foremost a moral philosopher, and later the founder of modern economics), tried to reconnect prudence to morality.

An entire section of his opus, *The Moral Theory of Sentiments*, is devoted to the virtue of prudence as a form of common sense. Thinking as he did about the rising wealth of nations, Smith transformed the concept of prudence into both an economic and a moral virtue.

Caution is not popular these days, and prudence in that sense is hardly the supreme virtue it once was, if it is a virtue at all.

No longer able to hold back gratification, modern individuals and governments cannot delay desire in the present—even if, in so doing, we could take steps to satisfy ourselves better later in time. Gratification must be instantaneous.

This is why our budgets are out of control and our debt is what it is.

Donald Trump, much like Ronald Reagan, is criticized by politicians on the left and the right for proposing solutions that are "too simple," not adequately thought out to meet the standard Washington think tanks demand of public policy wonks considered qualified to govern.

But for Trump, like Reagan, common sense was the core of public policy, demanding we ask of all government actions whether today's modern political excesses—such as a $20 trillion national debt—are prudent.

Put simply, if running a $20 trillion national debt is a bad idea, then to political thinkers of Reagan's or Trump's ilk, it only makes sense to take prudent measures to bring the national debt into a more manageable level, perhaps now, before paying interest on the national debt begins taking one-third or more of the federal budget.

Commonsense conservatism rooted in the virtue of prudence is making a comeback because Trump, like Reagan, is calling into question our political purpose and system of cronyism, victimization and entitlement.

It is high time for some more common sense and less immediate gratification, a principle Reagan and Trump would both see as antithetical to the prudent management of government.

UNDERSTANDING TRUMP AS A
PRINCIPLED POLITICIAN

There are those who seek merely to decry Trump, and there are those who are befuddled by him. His opponents want to destroy him now that he is winning, and some in the establishment—like former presidential candidate Mitt Romney and the old guard—fear his taking over the GOP.

Donald Trump and the political phenomenon he has created are most understandable.

Three kinds of people are involved in politics: political theorists, unprincipled actors, and principled actors.

POLITICAL THEORISTS

Theorists of both the right (like Charles Krauthammer and George Will) and the left (Brookings Institute senior fellow William Galston and Harvard University political theorist Danielle Allen) and many lesser minds in academia and in the media conceive of politics as putting into practice a preconceived theory.

To be educated into this ideology is to be taught how to expound, defend, and implement the ideology. Today, political theorists on both the left and the right act as if they believe their political goals can be advanced and largely accomplished through intellectual discourse alone.

Theorists expect politicians to be imperfect but deferential versions of themselves. The theorists like to be consulted, and while theorists may pretend they have no ego (it's all about the theory), political theorists today are increasingly devoted to maintaining and building their own prestige.

Political theorists believe that political actors who do not play their intellectual game are either fools or scoundrels.

Republican theorists pretend that Ronald Reagan was one of them. Reagan was great at giving speeches, even though he did not write many of them. In contrast, Abraham Lincoln wrote great speeches. But from the public record, many of Lincoln's speeches when first delivered were for one reason or another not fully appreciated. So, while Reagan may have been better at delivering great speeches and Lincoln was better at writing great speeches, both were first and foremost consummate politicians, not unduly constrained by any theory articulated in their public addresses.

The point is, both Reagan and Lincoln understood that the essence of politics is about action, not about theory, no matter how eloquently articulated.

UNPRINCIPLED ACTORS VS PRINCIPLED POLITICAL ACTORS

The Clintons epitomize what we mean in defining consummate unprincipled political actors, so much so that the definition of unprincipled political actors is today clear to most political observers without further elaboration.

When the Clintons are asked to express a vision, we get crafted phrases, such as "building a bridge to the twenty-first century," or a vision defined in personal terms, such as "first female president," which reduces to the assertion that politics is all about me.

Unprincipled political actors pursue politics in hopes of becoming wealthy celebrities capable of doing almost anything imaginable, without serious concern for morality, simply to win.

An unprincipled political actor will never emulate Harry S. Truman, who as president removed from his wallet a postage stamp he purchased to "frank" personal messages sent to keep in touch with family and friends back home in Independence, Missouri—the location to which he aspired to retire after serving his term in office as head of state.

Principled political leaders do not see politics as an end but as a means—a means to create, maintain or defend a way of life. It's the way of life that matters because principled political actors derive their satisfaction from real-world activities in private life. The classical examples are Lucius Quinctius Cincinnatus in the ancient world and George Washington in the modern world, two gentlemen who aspired to retire to their country estates, where they could resume their lives tending the land when the demands of politics no longer called them forth into the public arena.

Principled political actors do not need to be president or to see their photograph on the cover of *GQ* or *Vogue* to feel their lives are fulfilled.

DONALD TRUMP

Donald Trump can claim success in many fields of real-estate endeavor.

His vision, to make America great again, sounds corny to political theorists of the left who are so embarrassed at America's might and economic power that they gravitate to the hate America crowd. At the same time, his vision grates on political theorists on the right because Trump is unafraid to embrace big government when big government helps him advance toward his goal of making America great again.

Then, too, his willingness to be flexible in the world of realpolitik equally annoys political theorists on the left and on the right.

Trump exudes self-confidence, a confidence that comes in part from past achievement.

His assertion of self-confidence—"I'm number one in the polls"—as well as his assertion he is a billionaire financing his own campaign, embarrasses principled political actors who think humility is the sine qua non required for entry into the political pantheon. At the same time, these same assertions grate upon unprincipled political actors loathe to admit any other politician might be their superior, deserving of more public attention in the spotlight of celebrity.

For all three traditional definitions of political politicians—political theorists, principled political actors and unprincipled political actors—the real problem is that Trump believes it is true American can be great again, and he dares to say without any reservation that he has the talent and the means to accomplish that goal, even if he must do so against all odds.

For Trump, to exude confidence not only inspires others to confidence, but becomes a self-fulfilling act. But the truth is that to make America great again, one has to believe that one is a partial expression of that greatness. Trump wants all Americans to be included in that greatness he sees as possible for America, and he dares to extend his reach beyond party, class, race, gender, and region.

In this sense Trump has much to share with both Reagan and Lincoln in that all three gentlemen have embraced the highest ideals of our Founding Fathers with the naiveté to believe their destiny was to assist this nation in fulfilling that dream.

In the final analysis, Trump—like Reagan and Lincoln before him—loves America and welcomes the challenge to return this country to the glory our forefathers intended to bequeath to future generations. In the final analysis, Trump can embrace this challenge in this age because he is, after all, an entrepreneur.

A race between Hillary Clinton and Donald Trump will post an unprincipled politician against a principled one—with neither qualifying as political theorists. That much should be clear.

What remains harder for many on the left and on the right to grasp is that understanding Trump is really not all that difficult, not after you realize that Trump might actually achieve what he says he wants to achieve.

TRUMP'S VOICE FOR THE VOICELESS:

A NEW MAJORITY

After his resounding win in South Carolina, it is worth asking why Donald Trump is winning so resoundingly and will now likely become the Republican presidential nominee. To whom exactly is Trump giving voice?

In addition to the nearly constant personal attacks on Trump himself, the largest segment of his followers has themselves now come under rebuke. Although we shall not discuss them below, we want to acknowledge and emphasize that his supporters come from all walks of life, every community, ethnic group, gender, age and every race. The segment we wish to address is the so-called white working and middle class (WWMC)—52 percent of all Americans in 2015. This is, to use a phrase employed by Coolidge and then Nixon, Trump's "silent majority."

This segment of the US population is attacked from the left (*Huffington Post* and almost all mainstream media) for supposedly being xenophobic and racist. It is attacked from the right (*WSJ*) as being ignorant of economics and intolerant.

Let's look first at the charge of xenophobia. Rather than hating foreigners, what the WWMC experiences at the gut level is fear, anxiety, and distress at the erosion of American spiritual capital and the American dream. While the WWMC bases these conclusions on life experience, the same phenomenon has been identified at the scholarly level by Samuel Huntington (*Who Are We?*), Capaldi and Malloch (*American Spiritual Capital*), and Charles Murray (*Coming Apart*).

The essence of spiritual capital is high achievement and reward based on self-reliance, hard work, and faith in a transcendent being, which created America as an *exceptional* place, a New Jerusalem, a shining city on a hill. It welcomes all people who come to America to share that dream—not those who come to turn America, either wittingly or unwittingly, into the place from which they have just escaped. It welcomes ethnic food. (Thankfully we are no longer limited to the bland traditional British cuisine our Founding Fathers knew.) This vision of spiritual capital embraces everything that enriches America— rejecting the culture of poverty and pervasive cynical political corruption as a norm.

Unfortunately, under the guise of multiculturalism we see the erosion of American spiritual capital, the emptying of the melting pot and the substitution of belief in God for an intolerant secular humanism. The Democratic Party currently sees immigrants as recruits, to the detriment of the WWMC. But despite the revolutionary ambitions of the militant far left now controlling the Democratic Party, the WWMC is not defeated or discouraged. The genius of Trump is that his rhetoric, considered simplistic by the urbane, sophisticated far left of New York City and Hollywood, sees the American dream rekindled in Trump's enthusiasm. In Trump's assertion he will "make America great again," the WWMC sees hope a sound middle class income will once again be achievable in America, bringing with it the hope a secure future and a way forward for betterment may yet be attainable.

We move now to the charge of racism. There are lots of dysfunctional and wrongheaded people. How are we to understand them? Intellectual and media elites believe that everyone is a product of social circumstances beyond his/her control. As Harvard philosopher John Rawls once put it, those of us who are successful are products of the genetic lottery and happy family circumstances. If we work hard, that's only because of our DNA and ambitious parents (who in turn are products of their DNA and their ambitious parents, etc.). There is a total rejection on the part of elites of the idea that internalizing success norms is itself an act of free will and a serious commitment to postponing gratification. This is consistent with the determination of the secular elite on the far left today to write God out of the picture completely.

In writing God out of the equation, the moral responsibility of each human being is ruled out of any consideration for their success. That's where white guilt gets written into the picture as the central dynamics of the human equation. If some members of the minorities demand to be respected because they embraced the American dream and worked hard to overcome obstacles, they are to be ignored or charged with being Uncle Toms. The point of the far left is that white people succeed because white advantage is society's addition to DNA and happy family circumstances explaining why white people are more likely to be included in the famous "1 percent" of the economic heap the far left rails against.

The American dream is seen as a farce; the successful members of the WWMC are perceived to enjoy what is termed "white privilege." If there are dysfunctional people, they are to be pitied as victims who deserve an endless stream of resources, resources that do not go to the WWMC. The victims, of course, are the racial minorities and immigrants the far left of the Democratic Party sees as their constituents. When the WWMC objects to affirmative action they are called racist. When the WWMC is resentful of those who play the race card they are silenced by a pervasive PC political correctness.

We turn now to attacks launched upon the WWMC by the political right that controls the establishment GOP. Pundits aligning with George Will's brand of *Weekly Standard* conservatism believe that the WWMC is composed of economic nationalists, not *laissez-faire* economic actors in a free market economy. The free market is a great theory, but it does not exist in practice, certainly not in the international sphere—something that defenders of outsourcing tend to forget. It's easy to speak about the long-term benefits of a so-called free market when you are already a Washington insider benefiting from the increasing income inequality in America, in which WWMC chronically loses ground to cheaper foreign labor, whether accessed overseas through free-trade agreements or imported as illegal immigrants.

When Democrats are in control we get *crony* socialism; when the Republican establishment is in control we get *crony* capitalism. The pharmaceutical industry is an interesting case in point, switching from crony capitalism when it blocked Hillarycare, to crony socialism when it embraced Obamacare.

Republican elites—who routinely make six- and seven-figure incomes, who benefit from "insourcing" (looking the other way when the domestic economy encourages illegal immigrants to work here at less than market rates rather than in their native country), who move effortlessly in a cosmopolitan cultural bubble far removed from the WWMC, who politely ignore affirmative action because their kids will get into the Ivy League anyway, who live in expensive gated communities, who really don't care about the fate of minorities (they'll vote for the Democrats no matter what), who are willing to pander to activist Hispanics—think they will get enough of the WWMC vote by throwing a bone to a few evangelicals (having learned nothing from Mitt Romney's defeat).

While the supporters of socialist Bernie Sanders, especially the entitlement generation, want free stuff, supporters of Donald Trump in contrast want rewarding jobs. While the Washington elite in the George Will/*Weekly Standard* club hate labor unions, Donald Trump can claim to have hired in his various companies over decades more racial minorities and Latinos that all the other GOP presidential candidates put together. What a surprise it will be both to the current far-left establishment of the Democratic Party and the current William F. Buckley-descended "conservative" elite of the GOP when Donald Trump attracts the support of the "Reagan Democrats" that constitute a large percentage of today's WWMC.

What the Trump supporters from the WWMC want is simply restoration of the American dream! They seek a voice for the "silent majority." Truthfully, the American dream is bigger than any party or establishment, and it is more important than a narrow neoconservative ideology that loses elections and too often establishes only itself and the special interests that support it. The WWMC class needs a voice. Trump is the messenger of this voiceless group.

PRESIDENT TRUMP'S LIMITED
GOVERNMENT

In the preamble to the United States Constitution, the phrase "a more perfect union" is employed to describe the purpose for creating government. That phrase has at times been misconstrued and inappropriately applied.

Recall when then candidate Obama used it is a speech in Philadelphia by that very name to steer free of his former pastor, Rev. Jeremiah Wright, who had "goddamned America." Obama wanted to get past race baiting and free himself from the shackles of language, which would have plagued his campaign. Ironically, such "damning" has come to embody his entire presidency.

But what is the real meaning of limited government? It should be defined as a "system in which legalized force is restricted through delegated and enumerated powers." In other words, it is the exact opposite of what we have experienced over the last eight years.

This idea stems from *classical* liberalism, free (economic) markets, and conservatism in the earliest days of the United States. Bound by the Constitution, it systematically maintains principles of action that are spelled out in that Constitution. In the United States, this idea of limited government originated specifically in the notion of separation of powers and a system of checks and balances.

The Bill of Rights, in the Ninth and Tenth Amendments, outline once and for all and in clear, unambiguous terms, what the principles of limited government implied, i.e., the enumerated rights of the people versus the expressly delegated powers of the federal government.

Limited government, you see, stands in harsh contrast to the older doctrine of Divine Rights of Kings (or modern-day executives, presidents for life, dictators, klepocrats or the Clintons) where the king or executive alone holds *unlimited* sovereignty over his subjects.

Eight centuries ago we saw the major milestone and turning point in Western civilization, the Magna Carta. It remains the exemplar of a doctrine *limiting* the reach of sovereignty. But it was only in 1787, and in the United States Constitution, that we witnessed a government limited by the terms of the written document itself, the election of legislators by the people, and balancing the three branches of government by each other's powers.

In limited government, the power of government to intervene in the exercise of civil liberties is restricted by law. Government, by definition, cannot mandate equality through regulation of property and wealth redistribution. Reread the Federalist Papers, if in doubt. Madison, writing as Publius, made this case.

So the pertinent question today is: Does presidential candidate Donald Trump believe in and will he respect the tradition of limited government?

His words are as forthright as Madison's and embody a resounding yes.

Trump is a *strict* constitutionalist and has no expectations to usurp power or to grow the government. To the contrary, he has said he will give more powers and redirect funding to the states and use checks and balances as they were *originally* conceived. He will limit both his own executive powers and ask Congress and the courts to do the same. In other words, power will be returned "to the people." This is the kernel of Trump's populism, and it is as basic as the Boston Tea Party or the shots fired in Lexington by farmer militiamen.

All said, Trump's government will be smaller, more efficient, more frugal and use management principles and best practices, so as to be more excellent, i.e., we will actually get the services for which our hard-earned tax monies were contributed.

Under Trump, we will see limited government for the first time in sixty years.

Trump himself has said, "Common sense tell us that the two basic principles of governing should work anywhere they are applied. First: Get government out of activities it can't do well. (A list of thing government doesn't do well is a very long list.) Second: Get government back in the business of providing for public convenience (transportation and public works) and safety (police and firefighters), and make sure it does so efficiently. Then judge its efforts by visible, definable results and fine-tune, as needed."

Remember Donald Trump has self-funded his presidential campaign, disavowed PACs (no one else has) and is the puppet of no one or special interest. He complains constantly about "government incompetence" and cronyism. He promises "great management" of the limited government we need. He would employ all the skills from the private sector and deliver. As an entrepreneur, a doer, and a builder, he would allow every American to succeed, so as to make America great, again.

That narrative means limited government and maximum prosperity. Such a powerful combination would work to achieve what America's founders intended.

Those Founding Fathers knew it wasn't government that bestowed rights upon the American people. They firmly held that it was God who gave these rights to men, and as such they cannot be regulated, legislated or taken away by any man.

The founding was greatly influenced by the philosopher John Locke. Locke advocated government as a social contract. The term "will of the governed" summarizes this concept, and it was meant to show that the American people are the directors of those elected, *not* vice versa.

The power of the people is declared in the first three words of our Constitution, "We the People." This principle is also the underlying basis for the Declaration of Independence, which is revealed in these words:

> Governments are instituted among men, deriving their just powers from the consent of the governed. That whenever any form of government becomes destructive to these ends, it is the right of the people to alter or to abolish it, and to institute new government, laying its foundation on such principles and organizing its powers in such form, as to them shall seem most likely to effect their safety and happiness.

Trump would reinstitute limited government in America.

THE CANDIDATE WHO'LL RESTORE US

SPIRITUAL CAPITAL

I know a thing or two about the presidency and US presidents. This next election in November 2016 is a critical and historic crossroads for our country. We desperately need new leadership. Historically, America is a center-right polity and the modern exemplar of the Judeo-Christian heritage of "spiritual capital." Let me present two theses in this regard and demonstrate what they mean for presidential selection.

The first thesis concerns the logic of modernity. What distinguishes modernity is the Technological Project, the transformation of nature for human betterment as opposed to fatalistic conformity. This project requires inner-directed individuals and free-market economies that maximize competition and innovation. Free-market economies operate best with limited government (Montesquieu's "commercial republic" and Madison's *Federalist* No. 10). Limited government can only be maintained under the rule of law. The rule of law can only be sustained if there is a larger cultural context that celebrates responsible individual autonomy. Finally, responsible individual autonomy presupposes a larger ontological claim about human freedom or free will that requires a theological argument. Moreover, personal autonomy avoids self-destruction and adds a spiritual content to our development when the responsible use of freedom leads to helping to fulfill God's plan—by eliminating suffering and promoting freedom in and for others.

Recognizing, pursuing and sustaining such autonomy are

the spiritual quests of modernity, and this Project is best evidenced in the American experiment. The ultimate rationale for the Technological Project is not simply material comfort or consumer satisfaction, important as these are, but the production of the means of accomplishment. To discover that our greatest sense of fulfillment comes from freely imposing order on ourselves in order to impose a creative order on the world is perhaps the closest way of coming to know God.

Three considerations lead to the conclusion that America must maintain responsible personal autonomy. But all require deep support. First, personal autonomy presupposes free will. This amounts to saying that there is no naturalistic (and scientific) explanation of the ultimate truths about *who* we are. Second, we understand ourselves as historical beings, but history does not form a self-explanatory system. Our interpretation of the whole human drama depends on an intimately personal decision concerning the part we mean to play in it. In the end, this is a religious decision, not a scientific or academic one. Finally, sustaining our autonomy under trying circumstances requires spiritual stamina. Since naturalism and scientism fail, spirituality in some important sense emerges as the only discipline that can provide ultimate comprehension. Americans have long known and practiced this kind of faith.

The second thesis is the documented history of how settlers, seeking religious freedom in the United States, brought precisely this larger view to America, nourished it and sustained it. This is our legacy and destiny as a nation.

The most important historical development in the last four hundred years has been the rise of the Technological Project. This Project, not just the market, is the starting point for our

American narrative, because, although there have always been markets, it is only since the latter seventeenth century that markets have come to play such a dominant role in our lives. It is the presence of the Technological Project that explains the very centrality of those markets. America is first and foremost a land of opportunity, innovation and of growth.

This Project sees the control of nature for human benefit. It radically changed the way people in the West, and especially in America, viewed the world and their relationship to the world and led to fundamental changes in the major institutions of the West (economic, political, legal and social); this led to the expansion of the West and its relationship to the non-Western world, and finally to globalization—the internationalization of those Western institutions, including free markets and all they embody.

The following claims can be made:

- Technology is an irreversible historical fact. Abandonment of the Technological Project would have catastrophic consequences for humanity and threaten its very existence.

- To the extent that this Project creates environmental and other kinds of problems, we are now irrevocably committed to using future developments to address and hopefully solve those problems.

- Those cultures that have most fully embraced the Project (including military technology) have come to dominate the world and to spread its vision. This has not been a matter of the powerful imposing on the weak; the weak have largely (except for radical Islam) come to embrace the Project on their own.

This leads to the following tension and paradox: Domestically, government is to maintain a low profile and passive supporting role for commerce and order, but in the international context the government is to promote actively the entire panoply of the Technological Project, free-market economies, limited government and the rule of law. To act in foreign affairs to bring about this result is incumbent upon free governments. It is no use pretending that the implications could be otherwise.

The *next* president of the United States must abide by and within the established heritage of America's long-established spiritual capital. He or she cannot deny it, reject it, or pretend it away, as has been the case for Barack Obama. The democratic ideal of "interventionist socialism" and anti-Americanism we have toyed with over the last eight years surely must come to an end, as it is totally at odds with the essence of America's true spiritual capital.

Which of the Republican candidates on offer, then, *best* articulates America's spiritual capital in all the senses here described? This is the real question for voters.

Dismissing those who cannot be elected or do not have the funding or backing to lead or be elected, we are left with but a few choices. In my opinion, Donald Trump is the leader to endorse and choose. All of us, not just conservatives, need to rally behind him now—as America's *national* candidate. He alone has the business acumen; he alone has the executive experience; he alone is not polluted by Washington insider games; he alone articulates all of the necessary ingredients here spelled out. He best understands the Technological Project, the free economy of markets, the rule of law, and the limits to government. He wants to bring America back to its spiritual moorings and in his own words, *make it great again!*

Is his quiet religious faith an impediment? I think not. According to the leading sociologist of religion, when a religious habit continues for hundreds years it becomes an established fact. Trump embodies this uniquely American phenomenon. The US Constitution forbids any religious test for office holders. But a personal Christian faith is as American as apple pie. Protestants, evangelicals, Catholics, and Jews, all who have themselves often been persecuted for living their faith, should realize this more than any others. Under Donald Trump, there will no longer be any fear for loving God and worshiping in the open way Americans have long enjoyed. There will certainly be no theocracy, but America's spiritual capital will be renewed.

We desperately need a new leader, one in America's best spiritual tradition, to get us through the current malaise, a long battle with radical Islamism and economic chaos. We should choose well and use the framework here laid out to inform that choice.

3

THE OPPONENT(S)

HILLARY MISERY 2020

The famous economist, Arthur Okun, to calculate how bad things are for everyday Americans, created what he called the "Misery Index."

It is calculated by adding together the inflation rate and the unemployment rate as measured by the US Bureau of Labor Statistics. The number generally characterizes the current economic condition.

Empirically, a high unemployment rate and a high inflation rate have a negative impact on economic growth.

Recall in 1980 when President Carter was swept from office by conservative candidate Ronald Reagan, who asked the American people one simple question: "Are you better off than you were four years ago?"

Watch the video of that famous query if you have forgotten it.

Well, you may ask, how bad can things get looking into the crystal ball of the future? What would things look like in 2020 under a Hillary Clinton administration? Would there be more or less misery than we experience today?

President Obama's present Misery Index stands at 9.41, not as horrid as Carter's at 16.26, or even Gerald Ford's for that matter, but nothing to brag about. In fact, it is poor by comparison to most presidencies, and economic growth has been anemic to say the least. When it comes to job creation, Obama has been a disaster.

What would Hillary provide by 2020? Realistically, how bad could things get?

Recent research in technical economics shows that unemployment is much more closely correlated with unhappiness than inflation. Underweighting the effects attributed to unemployment rates is therefore politically and economically dangerous. Would Hillary be able to establish sustained economic growth?

And here is what we know about the present unemployment rate. It is not good if measured correctly as the labor *participation rate*, given that so many people and youths have actually dropped out of the economy altogether.

We have more than 93 million unemployed persons in the United States and 47 million people on food stamps. In other words, unemployment looks *much* worse than the numbers behold. In the African-American and Hispanic communities, and especially among youths, the rate is extremely high.

So the question Donald Trump needs to ask of Hillary Clinton at the debates this fall and on the campaign trail between now and then is this: *How miserable will she make the American people by 2020?*

Let's list the ways Clinton misery would rise:

- Her tax plan will raise taxes and hurt middle-class Americans in the pocketbook.

- Her trade polices (and new deals) will cost the country new job creation while shipping jobs overseas and to Mexico.

- Her health-care regime will keep people from affordable health and continue to raise the cost under an extended Obamacare.

- Her military policies will cost Americans their safety and make vulnerable our national defense.

- Her economic policies will keep the unemployment rates in terms of participation high and fail to create badly needed economic growth.

- Her business over-regulation and taxation will stop companies from building new facilities and expanding.

- Her open immigration policies will continue to let droves of illegal aliens cross our borders unabated. And

- Her foreign policy and lack of a strategy to defeat radical Islamic extremism and ISIS (she barely utter those words) will threaten our ability to function as a society as well as our personal security.

By the year 2020, America will be poorer, sicker, and more terrorized and the economy will not have recovered. Our Misery Index, and our unhappiness as a result, will likely be the worst it has ever been.

What would a President Trump do to improve our Misery Index overall?

- He would change the tax regime, making it dramatically lower for individuals, the middle class, and corporations, thereby putting more money into circulation.

- He would curtail our current trade policies and cancel the problematic new deals, thereby bringing jobs back to our shores.

- He would end Obamacare and institute health savings accounts, providing better and more cost-effective insurance to Americans.

- He would build back our decimated military forces so as to defend the country.

- He would work in every possible way to increase jobs for all classes and colors of Americans and make the economy competitive.

- He would cut regulation and bring back companies that have relocated elsewhere for tax reasons.

- He would build a wall on the Mexican border and control illegal immigration. And

- He would completely destroy ISIS and radical Islamic terrorism by enacting a comprehensive strategy in intelligence, policing and coordinated rapid military action.

In 2020, which scenario would you prefer?
Taking a page from the Reagan playbook ask: *Will you be*

better off in four years under Hillary Clinton?

Do Americans want jobs, security and economic growth or more and deeper misery?

Framed this way, Donald Trump defeats Hillary Clinton and we restore America's greatness. He says he wants to be the jobs president. That is what we need: more, good, high-paying and rewarding jobs.

Failure to vote on the part of the electorate—and that means *every* American voter, as an act of responsible citizenship—will doom us to greater misery by 2020. We will have no one to blame but ourselves.

Never before in American history have the stakes been so high or the choice so clear. Our very future as an economy, as a people, as a country, depends on it.

AMERICA IS HOME TO TWO
WORLD-CLASS KLEPTOCRATS

According to dictionary definitions, *kleptocracy* comes from the Greek word: *kleptēs* for thief, and *kratos,* for "power" or "rule"—hence "rule by thieves."

It is a term that can be applied to a government seen as having a particularly severe and systemic problem with officials or a ruling class, those called *kleptocrats*, taking from the people and gaining for themselves.

The Hudson Institute, a well-known DC think tank founded in 1961 that conducts innovative research on global security and prosperity, recently started a Kleptocracy Initiative. It actually measures the extent of such thievery. It analytically looks at the threat posed by autocracy, especially the financial practices of such regimes.

For them, kleptocracy is a system in which national economies are exploited for the illicit enrichment of a well-connected elite.

In other words, such regimes promote widespread, systemic corruption—affecting the lives of citizens, and threatening individuals and institutions.

The Kleptocracy Archive, is a free online database of documents that Hudson has developed illustrating the malfeasance emanating from corrupt authoritarian regimes.

You can view the entire archive here. It is most illustrative and well documented.

In history, the worst kleptocrats, according to the *Guinness*

World Records book, which keeps such records, have included this notorious list:

- President Suharto, president of Indonesia from 1967 until 1998, when his regime was overthrown, was the world's biggest kleptocrat. That is a person who thieves from his government. Transparency International estimated that he had stolen $35 billion.

- Ferdinand Marcos, president of the Philippines from 1972–86, $10 billion.

- Mobutu Sese Seko, president of Zaire from 1965–97, $5 billion.

- Sani Abacha, president of Nigeria from 1993–98, $5 billion.

- Slobodan Milosevic, president of Serbia/Yugoslavia from 1989–2000, $1 billion.

- Jean–Claude Duvalier, president of Haiti from 1971–86, $800 million.

- Alberto Fujimori, president of Peru from 1990–2000, $600 million.

- Pavlo Lazarenko, prime minister of Ukraine from 1996–97, $200 million.

- Arnoldo Alemán, president of Nicaragua from 1997–2002, $100 million.

- Joseph Estrada, president of the Philippines from 1998–2001, $80 million.

It has been reported that India's Gandhi family, considering all branches, likely has stolen in the hundreds of billions of dollars, most of which is hidden in accounts in Switzerland.

Putin and the Saudis and other Middle Eastern thieves should arguably also be on this list, as could other older despots, but inflation has swelled the numbers for the top 10 and you could say—it is their oil, after all.

Russian thievery is arguably a whole separate category, and Putin and his Kremlin gang have literally looted the entire country, allegedly making him perhaps the richest person in the world.

What about our own *homegrown* kleptocrats? Should we not place the Clintons at the very top of the list, given the established facts that they went from humble civil servants to a net worth of some $245 million in short order? And they used the illegal and corrupt mechanism of their hydra-like charity, whose principal public face to the world since mid 2013 is called the Bill, Hillary, and Chelsea Clinton Foundation.

How much money have donors sent to the Clinton Foundation?

The truth is, no one actually knows.

Though applicable laws demand that US charities, such as those run by the Clintons, make timely and granular public disclosures, no Clinton charity has ever done so since October 1997, when the original tax-exempt entity set out to build a presidential archive and research facility in Bill Clinton's home state of Arkansas.

No competent and independent accounting firm has ever verified how much money donors sent to the Clinton Foundation since inception, or what the Clintons and their associates did with contributed donations.

That said, press releases, glossy brochures, and unvetted financial disclosures report considerable activity—cumulative declared inflows to the Clinton Foundation from 1997 through 2014 exceed $2 billion, while cumulative outflows during the same period are stated to be approximately $1.8 billion.

Judging from Clinton Foundation disclosures, the overwhelming majority of activity had nothing to do with the original authorized purposes of being a Little Rock presidential archive.

Beginning in January 2001, shortly after the Clintons left the White House, Bill Clinton began raising funds in the name of his foundation ostensibly to pursue myriad causes as far flung as relief of natural disasters, fighting HIV/AIDS and arresting adverse impacts of "climate change."

There is no readily available evidence in the public domain that Bill Clinton and others responsible for oversight *ever* validly obtained authorization to so radically alter focus of the Clinton Foundation, from the chief government overseer of US charities—the US Internal Revenue Service.

This brings us to one element of the Clinton Foundation that started operating by September 2005 the (so-called charitable) Clinton Global Initiative that claims to be a charity but, instead, seems to serve as vehicle where the Clinton family and their associates likely sell influence and peddle access while in power.

To see how much potential there has been to engage in activities that are far from being "charitable" and more likely means to market products and services, and concoct business and investment transactions with powerful government leaders, take a close look through the searchable database of Commitments to Action found at clintonfoundation.org/clinton-global-initiative

/commitments. These are unenforceable indications of intent to pursue supposed good works that do not appear to be monitored by any competent and independent overseer or regulator in any meaningful way.

Likely by design, there is no way to tell how much charitable good work truly gets performed and how much Clinton Global Initiative contributors gain, by comparison, from pursuing projects gained under the cover of philanthropy.

Would eight more years of Clinton rule not push a family that was literally "dead broke" in January 2001 to the top of the all time *earnings* list?

Look at these facts: We now know that the Saudi government has donated some $25 million to the Clintons: Qatar, $5 million; Kuwait, another $5 million; and $17.7 million has been given from other foreign governments.

During Clinton's tenure as secretary of state, the Foundation operated in at least twenty-nine countries, including places that contained rampant corruption—such as Nigeria, Uganda, Ukraine, Haiti, Mozambique, China, and South Africa.

The Clinton duo is a world-class kleptocratic machine taking from the world's worst regimes to enrich *themselves*. This is what American democracy has stooped to. How much lower can it go? Wait and see.

Now the antidote to kleptocracy is twofold: *transparency*, so the citizens of the whole world can see for themselves what is being stolen, by whom, and to what end, and *penalty*.

The United States and like-minded democratic countries seriously interested in good governance, if that is not an oxymoron, need to enforce a rule.

Any funds stolen from the people and deposited anywhere in

the world to the inurement of any kleptocrat must be returned, with interest. The kleptocrats should then be charged and sentenced for felony—or should we say, grandest larceny with a fine triple to the funds stolen and lifetime imprisonment.

You can go to Yale, or you can go to jail. Oh, the Clinton's could do both!

"PARDON ME," HILLARY ASKS,
"UNTIL I CAN PARDON MYSELF"

The word *pardon*, as a kind indulgence, as in forgiveness of a slight offense, discourtesy, or inconvenience, is well worn. As an excuse, asking for pardon (as in "pardon, me") is rather commonplace in our everyday lives.

But in law a pardon has a much more dire meaning, as release from the actual penalty of an offense, or a remission of a crime by some authority—be it a governor, president or even the pope. Indeed, this involves forgiveness of a far more serious sort.

This idea of release from penalty originated in the thirteenth century with the papal indulgences and the Old French "par don" or Latin *perdonare* to give a remit. Pardons became a big business; they were sold and traded.

Today our presidents can circumvent the justice system by issuing official pardons of their choosing, granting clemency, as it is known. Such acts cannot be altered by Congress, cannot be reviewed, blocked or overturn. The most controversial pardons in US history have included: the whiskey rebels, Brigham Young, confederate soldiers, Eugene Debs, Jimmy Hoffa, Richard Nixon, Patty Hearst, and Marc Rich.

Fast-forward to the American political scene in the present frame. Candidate Hillary Clinton, the ultimate Washington insider and Democratic Party front-running candidate to be the next president, is both asking for and needs numerous pardons. Will the American people give her a pass? Will the justice system overlook possible criminal violations?

She is saying, "Pardon me for my slightest of mistakes or oversights. I did not mean any harm when, as I told the congressional committee, we were just trying to deal with the complex Benghazi events. I never meant to hurt anyone—not the ambassador, nor the security guards, and certainly not poor Susan Rice, whom I knowingly sent onto the weekend television shows to tell a falsehood to cover my tracks."

Hillary's request to be pardoned does not stop there.

"Pardon me for Libya and for the birth of ISIS," she says, noting that she is not allowed to call it Islamic terrorism, as that would offend many Muslims.

"I never imagined such could flow from the Arab Spring," Hillary continues. "That was supposed to go, oh so differently. It was always intended to be a democracy movement, wasn't it?"

"Well, I can always blame it on David Cameron or the Europeans, as President Obama, the anointed One, did recently in The Atlantic magazine," she pleads. "It wasn't my fault or his! Besides, it was Bush that started this whole mess. When in doubt I always blame Bush. It's so easy to have a scapegoat that you almost don't need to ask for a pardon at all."

"On Obamacare, remember, I am the original author and chair of the task force that devised the plan 'Hillarycare,' as my detractors called it officially the Health Security Act of 1993, during my husband's presidency. That led to our massive congressional defeat in 1994 and the 'Contract with America,' which changed American politics, shifting power in the House of Representatives to the Republicans after a long forty years in the dark. Thank you, Newt Gingrich and Dick Armey for that disservice."

Hillary continues, asking for even more pardons.

"Pardon me for not being harder on my predator and sex-addicted husband, Bill, who, as we know from the television drama 'House of Cards,' is wedded to me not as a betrothed marriage partner, so much as a political partner," she argues. "I stood by my man on *60 Minutes* long ago so he could win. Now, he will do the same for me so I can win."

"I am no feminist, so I guess you will have to excuse all my actions in the war on women," she reasons. "Really, Bill can't help himself, as we know from the sordid intern-affair with what's her name—but I did look the other way to enable him."

"I ask your pardon as well for an embarrassing defeat in 2008 in the primaries to that black candidate I tried to smear," she notes. "Even Bill calling Barack a fantasy came to no avail. Look, we did not mean any racial slur. You see, I supported Barack in victory and even served his administration for four years.

"But it is the legal sense of pardon that I now plead, so I can advance to my lifelong dream of capturing the White House," she concludes.

"Frankly, I need a pardon in that strictest sense from both Attorney General Lynch and from my former boss, President Obama, as soon as possible and certainly before November's election.

"I need it to get me off the hook for my HUGE violation of US laws regarding the use of a private email server routed through my private residence, violating numerous federal laws, where classified information was compromised," she insists, expressing determination.

"Just in case the FBI calls for my imminent indictment, I, Hillary Clinton, need to cash in a big IOU with President Obama. Please, pretty please, do pardon me," she asks, showing real emotion. "I promise, Mr. President, that after this one last pardon, I'll never need to ask again. After all, once I'm president, I can pardon myself whenever I need to do so."

Then she paused, having one last thought.

"And when I leave office," she says, with glee, "I grant my self a future pardon, for any and all crimes and misdemeanors I might commit some time, or any time, in the future. If I'm really clever, I'll pardon myself into eternity, making it a whole lot easier when finally I encounter St. Peter there, waiting at the Pearly Gates to allow me entry."

OBAMA'S "FINAL VICTORY" TOUR:

A GLOBAL THUGFEST

The forty-fourth president of the United States, Barrack Hussein Obama, entering his last year as a "lame duck" holder of the White House, has evidently decided to begin a final victory lap with the Castro brothers in Cuba, appearing now with the gray hair we have come to expect from every aging rock star seeking to bow out with a run of concerts on a farewell tour.

Obama has already announced he would equally like to visit Tehran before he leaves office, adding the Islamic Republic of Iran to the list of US enemies the president somehow still believes he can charm into civility.

In two terms as president, Obama arguably has implemented an economic policy that has increased economic disparity between the rich and poor, while capping off his domestic policy with attacks on the police and support for groups on the radical left like Black Lives Matter that have left race relations at a level of conflict that was inconceivable when the Voting Rights Act was signed into law in 1964.

With regard to foreign policy, Obama has dramatically reduced the strength of America's military, while refusing to utter the words "radical Islamic terrorism" as he performs the wave with Raul Castro at a baseball game where he gives his only interview on the terrorist bombings in Brussels to ESPN.

Overall, it has been quite a prize-winning achievement, as the Russian military intervenes in Syria, ISIS throws the Middle East into crisis and Iran test fires intercontinental ballistic missiles before the ink is dry on the much-touted nuclear agreement Secretary of State John Kerry negotiated releasing billions of dollars without requiring Tehran to abandon its "Death to Israel" rhetoric.

What ever happened to Obama's 2009 inauguration promise to "refurbish the US image abroad," especially in the eyes of Muslims, to end the war in Iraq and Afghanistan, and to "reset" relations with Russia? Obama has indeed bent the arc of history—and precisely in the opposite direction of his feeble and naïve words.

But maybe we are harsh in judging Obama as delusional in thinking his performance in office justifies a final victory lap tour. Maybe, just maybe, Obama's presidency has turned out precisely as he planned.

So, Obama's victory tour starts in Havana, Cuba, where Obama agrees that the Castro brothers probably have a legitimate gripe against the United States for John F. Kennedy overreacting, just because in 1962 Russia placed a few ballistic missiles armed with nuclear warheads on the island.

After declaring the Cold War with Cuba over, perhaps we are lucky Obama flew off to Argentina before he gave Gitmo away.

What countries might be next?

Obama might return to Africa, the continent of his father's birth, where he could meet with Zimbabwe's President Robert Mugabe, asking him to explain how he managed to get himself appointed president for life.

Before leaving Africa, Obama might spend a day in Pretoria and give his regards to ANC oligarch Jacob Zuma.

His next stop might be Paris, France, where Obama could

stand tall with Socialist President François Hollande, his firm ideological eco-buddy. Together, Obama and Hollande might celebrate the United Nations Climate Treaty for all its tax-increasing possibilities.

Certainly, Obama will visit eastern Ukraine with a side trip to Crimea, where he can toast with the invading Russian army. Obama will certainly want to acknowledge Putin's takeover of the region, while he stood by doing nothing.

Well, Obama had a golf game to work on, and Russians can be tough, you know. Remember Stalin?

After a brief but dangerous visit to Raqqa, in Syria, to meet with the people whose name he refuses to pronounce (ISIS), Obama attends a jihadist sharia court where his supposed acumen as a constitutional scholar could be put to some good use.

Avoiding Israel and its leader at all costs, Obama can fly from Syria over to visit the failed state Pakistan where he can review the Muslim-controlled nuclear weapons his administration could not eliminate the way he unilaterally reduced the US nuclear arsenal.

Flying to Korea, Obama can stop off for a one-on-one basketball game with his favorite dictator Kim Jung-un, working up an appetite for a state dinner as guest of the Democratic Republic of North Korea. Obama certainly will not mind if his host invites his good buddy Dennis Rodman to join them.

In Beijing, with strongman and Communist Party boss Xi Jinxing, Obama can wink-wink acknowledge that he meant no harm excluding China from the capstone of his presidency, the Trans-Pacific Partnership, explaining that his plan all along was to sell the TPP to Beijing once Congress fast-tracked it into law.

Landing Air Force One back on US soil, Obama could hold

a final victory tour rock concert in the East Room, inviting his special friends, including Weather Underground bomber Bill Ayers, his America-hating former pastor Rev. Jeremiah Wright, notorious money man George Soros and the always captivating Harry Reid.

On January 19, 2017, Obama can give his farewell address to the nation in which he can finally declare, "Mission Accomplished!"

On Inauguration Day, Obama can jet off to New York, where he can prepare for his next assignment as United Nations secretary-general, where he anticipates his next "four more years" can be spent causing perpetual gridlock in Midtown as he sets about accomplishing for the world community what he accomplished for the United States.

After all, in a General Assembly and Security Council where enemies are to be embraced as friends, where the words "radical Islamic terrorism" need never be articulated and where the most intransigent global problem can be solved by inserting the words "sustainable growth" into all accords, Obama can comfortably declare: "What, me worry?"

MIRROR, MIRROR, ON THE POLITICAL WALL...

We all know the tale of Snow White and the Evil Queen. It is etched into our literature, and thanks to Disney, into our cinematic memories. The origin of the story dates to the Brothers Grimm and is far more gruesome than the sanitized version we have come to know and adore.

But the newer version of that epic drama is even darker still and reads like this:

Mirror, Mirror, on the wall,

Who's the most crooked of them all?

And the resounding answer this political season is:

Hillary, Hillary —she is crooked beyond compare.

Donald Trump has in fact urged us to dub her, Crooked Hillary; and it sticks.

Let us name the ways she is *so* crooked. For it all goes back to those Seven Dwarfs (in PC language—they would simply have to be referred to as challenged little people) so consider this:

Like *Doc*, Hillary may be no medical doctor but she presumes she knows what's *best* for you—from healthcare to security and from welfare to income, she is the expert and knows best...or does she?

Like *Grumpy*, which has always meant, surly and ill tempered, Hillary does not like anyone who has the audacity to disagree with her. Look at poor, old Bernie Sanders or all the others in the Clinton graveyard.

Like *Happy*, which originally stemmed from being lucky, Hillary has positioned herself well—surrounded by her predatory husband and all the cronies she keeps happy and rich, her politics are rooted in a form of managerial capitalism, where you loot all you can (get away with).

Like *Sleepy*, Hillary puts us in a somnolent mood, her long, boring speeches dragging on and on and her pantsuits are a relic from the 1970s. Her time indeed, has come and gone.

Like *Dopey*, which means stupefied, either by sleep or a drug, Hillary is literally a dope when it comes to sleeping on the job, thereby drugging us to believe all her constant lies and lame excuses. She has no resume beyond the government—and most of that was what we call coattail work. She never ran anything and was gifted into positions.

Like *Bashful*, which actually in days of yore meant embarrassed and disconcerted, Hillary embarrasses the citizenry and never, ever accepts the blame for anything. And boy the list of misdeeds, illegalities, and errors is extensive, even criminal.

Like *Sneezy*, in Middle English this meant misreads, Hillary always misreads the public, and instead imposes her elite democratic socialist mentality on any given policy or need. She never saw a problem *more* government couldn't fix. Will the public finally catch on and read her correctly this time?

In his epic tome on political theory, the great Oxford thinker Isaiah Berlin popularized the idea of the "crooked timber of humanity." Hillary is, however, more crooked than the average, Tom, Dick, or Mary. She is as the mirror suggests, crooked beyond compare.

Truth be known, Berlin borrowed this idea from Immanuel Kant, who said long before (translated from German):

> Each of them will always abuse his freedom if he has none above him who exercises power in accord with the laws. The highest ruler should be just in himself, and still be a human. This task is therefore the hardest of all; indeed, its complete solution is impossible, for from such *crooked wood* as a human is made can nothing quite straight ever be fashioned.

The phrase is actually contained in his sixth thesis of the *Idea for a General History from a Cosmopolitan Perspective,* written in 1784, I am sure you are familiar with that neglected classic.

This notion of human depravity, the fall from grace, and of sin itself, was brought forward in the West by Saint Augustine based on a biblical interpretation of Genesis, chapter 1.

You remember from Sunday school how Adam and Eve broke God's promise in the Garden of Eden and ate the forbidden fruit—the apple of knowledge, thereby altering their (and our own) natures, forever.

Well, Hillary Clinton embodies the Genesis story more than any contemporary political person. She swallowed the whole thing and is corrupt beyond compare. Her politics are grim, grimmer than even the Brothers Grimm.

She should therefore be disqualified from ever becoming president because of her sin against the American people. God forgive her, no one else can. The mirror never lies, but rather beholds a truth.

HILLARY CLINTON *IS* GOLDMAN SACHS

Many, many days after promising to 'look into it,' the transcripts of Hillary Clinton's speeches to Goldman Sachs Investment firm were leaked online by an unknown source. Thank you.

Here's what Hillary actually said, Thank you, very much, Lloyd [Blankfein], and thanks to everyone at Goldman Sachs for welcoming me today. I'm delighted to be back among friends, colleagues, collaborators, supporters, kindred spirits."

In other words, she confirmed what we *all* expected: she is one of them—and a true kindred spirit. She is on their payroll.

Clinton went on to note,

> Previous generations of Americans built this economy and a middle class on a collective illusion: that they do productive work, this creates wealth, and that this builds the economy. We all know how misguided that is. We know that it's really due to your investing, credit, and economic stewardship, that they have been able to work at all, that they are able to put food on their tables. It's due to you and other banking, trading, investment houses that we have an economy that works at all. You are why we are a truly twenty-first century economic power.

Apparently, Clinton detests the middle class and its values, religious sentiments, and diligent work habits. She expressed the views of an elitist snob and a person who detests real wealth creation.

Clinton went on to speak about the revolt in the Sanders-leaning wing of her own political party and the populist effect of her likely opponent, one Donald Trump:

But I—contrary to populist, hysterical demonizing—firmly believe that what you do is essential and critical: you help allocate our investment, direct our economic development, hedge risks, and create power, policies, and alliances in ways that make our country stronger, richer, more powerful, more innovative, competitive, and yes, more "democratic."

You can read the speeches, for which Clinton received *$625,000* dollars as they are now posted onto the file-sharing site PasteBin.

To be fair, most of the speeches texts appear to be rather innocuous and glad-handing. Yes, Clinton did speak glowingly about Goldman Sachs, about how much money they make and what a great friend they are to her and her Super PAC. That after all is the vehicle she employed to indirectly pay for her costly campaign to defeat Bernie and run against, The Donald in the general election.

But there is one zinger of a quote from Hillary that should draw particular fire from any observers:

> But seriously, I believe that the work of Goldman Sachs is critical for us, and without you, America would be a faint shadow of its current greatness. It's fair to say that you have transformed the solid, clunky, friction-laden trading of traditional commodity speculation into responsive, intelligent, liquid flows, that have vaporized every barrier and transformed into an expansive, responsive, endlessly expanding gas that fills every atom of our productive economic space that generates immeasurable value everywhere it goes, and everything it touches. Who cares that it's a little chaotic or "unethical"?

This is the clincher and tell-all and the reason why she was paid a small fortune to make the speech and why she does not want the American public to see it. It is in a sense an IOU on future access and future policy.

> And so I say to you Goldman Sachs, *I am on your side. Do not pay attention to the noise of the political season, I will always remember your support and put your priorities first, above all else. Thank you.*

Clinton received the princely fee of *$675,000* for three speeches she made to Goldman Sachs in 2013 alone. That is the income of over twenty US families at present income levels.

It is often said, that you get what you pay for; and in this case, it is fair to say, Goldman Sachs *owns* her.

In the words of one of the Goldman employees who attended the speech, "I remember feeling like she worked for us." This person was at the event in Arizona in October of 2013. He went on to recount, "Now she's telling people what they want to hear so she can get elected. But back then it sounded to us like she was our employee."

At another speech to Goldman Sachs in New York, earlier in 2013, Hillary Clinton spoke about how the banks were not to blame for the financial crisis and that she would make sure, *that the American people would always bail them out "no matter what."*

Hillary not only believes in "too big to fail" but also endorsed a future bailout. She has a peculiar view of capitalism: privatize the massive Wall Street profits going to her political friends and cronies, and socialize their losses.

Hillary Clinton, the Democrat Party candidate to be president of these United States, was perhaps more corrupt, more dishonest, and more insidious than *any* candidate in the history of persons to run for the most powerful executive office in the land—indeed the whole wide world.

Here is how one listener concluded what he heard her say to Goldman Sachs.

"It felt like a generous tongue bath from a loving puppy, I can understand why she wouldn't want anyone to see the text of these speeches, it makes her look really corrupt."

In the Clinton's America, democracy is for sale, and she and her husband are the money collectors.

CLINTON: TOO BIG TO JAIL?

The phrase "too big to fail" refers to the theory that certain corporations, and particularly financial institutions, i.e., the biggest banks, are so large and so interconnected that their failure would be disastrous to the greater economic system. Government therefore must support them when they face potential failure, i.e., bailed out by the taxpayer.

Ever since the 2008 global financial crisis, opponents argue that the policy of bailing out such large institutions is in fact counterproductive because such institutions are likely to take riskier positions in the knowledge that they are going to be bailed out, and consequently bailing them out actually causes more widespread, longer-term recessions, than if they had been allowed to declare bankruptcy and been reorganized in the first place.

The "too big to fail" doctrine has become the slogan for privatizing profits and socializing losses of the big and well-connected banks.

More dangerous, however, may be the concept of "too big to jail," the public perception that someone who has committed a serious crime or crimes is allowed to go free because their wealth or political influence enabled them to bypass the justice system.

In America, the rule of law includes not only the concept that the law must be obeyed, but also the concept that everyone must obey it: the understanding that it applies equally to all, including the wealthy and including the government itself, and most especially, those who work for the government.

It is for this reason that Lady Justice is traditionally pictured as being blind.

The rule of law has been of fundamental importance to American society. Without it, without generalized respect for the law, our society would collapse and anarchy would reign. While we may not always live up to our foundational principles—such as "all men are created equal"—that does not mean that we should not strive to live up to them, and it does not mean that they are not necessary—for our very existence as a nation.

Recently, James B. Comey, director of the FBI, explained that his agency did not "find clear evidence that Mrs. Clinton or her colleagues intended to violate laws," even though she had acted in a way that was "extremely careless in the handling of very sensitive, highly classified, information."

He further stated that while he did not have direct evidence that 'hostile actors' (i.e. unfriendly foreign governments and agents) accessed Hillary's private email, he did find that such actors gained access to the e-mail accounts of people with whom Clinton was in regular contact. Thus, his implication was that then secretary of state Hillary Clinton allowed foreign powers to access US classified information by means of her unsecured personal email. Despite all of this, he concluded that "[a]lthough there is evidence of potential violations of the statutes regarding the handling of classified information, our judgment is that no reasonable prosecutor would bring such a case."

The statutes that make the mishandling of classified information a crime include 18 U.S.C. §§793(d), 798, 1924.

All three crimes include intent as an element of the crime.

Section 798 stipulates that whoever "knowingly and willfully" communicates or uses in any manner prejudicial to the safety or interest of the United States any classified information can be jailed up to ten years. Section 793 says the same about willfully communicating information relating to the national defense to someone not authorized, and Section 1924 stipulates that any officer of the United States who knowingly removes them or retains them without authority can be imprisoned for up to one year. Furthermore, 19 U.S.C. 2071 provides that anyone who has custody of US governmental records, which include official emails, and willfully and unlawfully conceals or removes them, shall be fined or imprisoned up to three years, and shall be disqualified from holding any official US office (which would ostensibly include the office of the president).

Hillary's methods of dealing with the information she received as Secretary of State clearly violated *all* of these statutes. Her use of an unsecured email server for sending and receiving classified information was prejudicial to the safety and interest of the United States and jeopardized its defense. Furthermore, she and her attorneys destroyed some thirty thousand emails, some of which were found by Mr. Comey to have concerned official business and contained classified information.

The issue, then, is whether her doing so was "intentional."

Criminal intent, or *mens rea,* has a number of definitions. Sometimes it is used to refer to a 'varying state of mind which is the contrary to an innocent state of mind.' Often it includes criminal negligence as well as actual intent to do harm. Occasionally, it includes an implication of knowledge of the law violated, but in general, such knowledge is not required for conviction: 'ignorance of the law is no excuse.'

In sum, intent means that the perpetrator intended to do the act, regardless of whether he or she knew it was a crime at the time.

Hillary claims that she did not remember that the State Department gave her explicit instructions on how to handle classified information at the time she ascended to her high office because she was suffering from the effects of a concussion. Nevertheless, Mrs. Clinton apparently intended to send classified information by way of her unsecured, personal email server—whether she knew that was a crime or not is irrelevant. (Though it strains credibility that she would *not* know that such information should only be sent by way of protected, encrypted US government servers, given her many years of experience as a US Senator and former First Lady).

Consequently, there is *prima facie* evidence that any good prosecutor could establish all elements of the several crimes of mishandling of classified information. Whether he or she could do so beyond a reasonable doubt may never be determined because the FBI (so far) has not recommended that she be prosecuted.

Guess why? Something happened when Bill Clinton met with the Attorney General Lynch on that coincidental visit on the runway in Phoenix and it stinks to high heaven. What happened: justice was thwarted!

However, there is a problem here: other, lesser government officials have recently faced trial and severe punishment for mishandling classified information.

Petty Officer First Class Kristian Saucier used a cellphone to take six photos in the engine room of the nuclear submarine where he worked. He did not transfer them to anyone, but unlawfully kept them on his cell phone, destroyed evidence relating to them, and then lied about it. He was sentenced to one year in prison and $100 fine.

CIA director and retired four-star general David Petraeus divulged classified information to his biographer/mistress. He was eventually sentenced to two years' probation and a fine of $100,000—in addition to having had to withdraw from his position in disgrace.

Both of them were punished in accord with the rule of law.

There is a difference between these two cases and Hillary Clinton's situation. Generally, members of the military such as Saucier and Petraeus are more likely to be prosecuted for mishandling classified information. The Justice Department usually does not prosecute a civilian employee of a federal agency (which is what Hillary Clinton was) as long as there is (1) no evidence of criminal intent, (2) the information was not disclosed to another party, and (3) the employee's supervisor thoroughly disciplined him or her.

The Justice Department once infamously prosecuted an innocent naturalized citizen and scientist, Wen Ho Lee, for allegedly giving nuclear secrets to the Chinese government, but it generally will not do so in the absence of the three criteria mentioned above.

However, *all* those three criteria are present here: there is evidence of criminal intent, the information was disclosed to another party, and Mrs. Clinton was not disciplined by her only superior—the president.

As the US secretary of state, Mrs. Clinton was the United States' chief diplomat and the president's chief advisor on foreign policy, one of the US's most powerful civil servants and could endanger our safety more easily than a lowly sailor, a nuclear scientist, or even the head of the CIA.

Her duty to the American people to protect secrets should

have been her overwhelming concern, and her failure to do so should at least lead to the Justice Department's consideration of whether or not she should be tried. The fact that she is not facing at minimum an indictment leads one inexorably to the impression that the FBI controls the Justice Department or is it *vice versa*, and that our Government is no longer blind and is instead politicized in favor of powerful Democrats who cover up crimes.

The fact that the FBI refuses to recommend that Hillary Clinton be similarly prosecuted flies in the face of the rule of law.

Ironically, one of those who began her career by trying to prove that president Nixon should be tried by the Senate for his illegal actions (whether she did so by honest means or not) is herself now—too big to jail.

KRUGMAN NEARLY ALWAYS WRONG

Paul Krugman, No. 1 opinion page editorialist for the *New York Times* and professor of (macro) economics at NYU, is really nothing more than a limousine liberal, champagne hatchet man for the Clinton's.

He should be seen for what he is, the most vocal supporter of Hillary for president. He goes out of his way in offending Bernie Sanders *and* Donald Trump, calling *both* of them "delusional."

Krugman has himself become very accomplished at one thing, namely: name-calling.

Paul Krugman won a Nobel Prize in economic science in 2008 for his earlier work on trade theory. He actually served in a junior position briefly on the Reagan Council of Economic Advisors—something he often hides. Nowadays, he is a leftist puppet that no longer uses economic science, preferring instead, inflammatory rhetoric.

Krugman has been decidedly wrong about the 1990s where *very* little shared prosperity was generated. He has been wrong about supply side feedbacks and about the benefits of globalization (unless you believe in the elevation of China's development).

He selectively chooses statistics (liars figure) instead of admitting that there has in fact been no boom for ordinary people. The numbers show that wages were flat in the 1990s for the bottom 90 percent of the US population and the whole thing died in 2001 in the dotcom crash, wiping out the supposed investment boom. I know too well, as I lost my shirt.

Those numbers have stagnated ever since or declined.

That's Dr. K's model: pontificate as a learned bearded

economist, when in truth you are nothing more than a shrill whore for the liberal establishment.

His solution for *every* problem is the same: raise taxes and have the federal government get further into debt. Twenty trillion is not enough for Paul, the ultimate proponent for spending *our* hard earned money on wasteful boondoggles and giveaways.

So condescending, Krugman has become a snide polemist that has given up on reason and economic argument. He is not an academic who uses objective factuality any longer but instead, is these days, a know it all—who knows very little.

Please recall however during the 2008 campaign, that the same Dr. Krugman hit on then candidate Barrack Obama, calling him a "hero of venom and a "cult of personality." He has seriously been the Clinton's bagman of ideas—forever.

Krugman is primarily interested in only one cult, his own. His overt biases make him both academically questionable and scientifically discredited. He gave a lecture in Oxford last year on the condition that no one could challenge his positions. Really this is academe? What kind of academy does Krugman need where everyone pays obeisance? However, at FreedomFest when he debated Steve Moore (from the *Wall Street Journal*, for a boatload of money), he lost.

Krugman is nothing more than an establishment ventriloquist in a cushy leather academic library chair paid for by some innocent donor who has been robbed. He has never run anything, served in a corporation or managed a profit & loss statement effecting real employees or been judged by the bottom line.

Yet this windbag is given a perch weekly in a notable newspaper to knock Trump because he lacks "management skills. " How would he know?

For Krugman success in business does *not* equal economic success.

Admittedly, partisan Krugman makes the constant statement that Democrats perform better without looking at the full set of statistics that disprove his slanted judgment. Calling people ignorant blowhards " is not the same as disproving their arguments or denying real facts.

Why do people like Krugman run down accomplished entrepreneurs like Trump, among others, who use the market and their considerable skills to extol not only the virtues of democratic capitalism but who demonstrate its beneficial effects on everyone in the value chain—from vendors and employees to communities and charities? The reason in a single word, actually a deadly vice, is: *envy.*

For Krugman there should never be a business leader.

President Hoover, who was as close as we have come, is made out to be a failure because the depression started in a stock market crash just months after his inauguration.

Krugman states this proposition: *CEOs don't know anything about running a national economy, which is nothing like running a business.* "Running the economy demands a macroeconomist, the likes of Krugman. Only such Keynesian wisdom and econometric modeling can comprehend the contours of this tangled global system. And they have done *so* well after all.

To quote Krugman, "The truth is that the idea that Donald Trump, of all people, knows how to run the US economy is ludicrous." Well, the *only* thing more ludicrous is that Krugman and his crony capitalist Goldman Sachs pony, Hillary Clinton, would be *more* qualified.

Krugman claims, as his book and column suggest, that he is,

"the conscience of liberalism." It might be better stated that he is the prophet of more and more government intervention and the precise reason that the left is failing. He and his ilk are, to steal a now familiar phrase, the culprits for why America is crippled.

In my humble opinion, Professor Krugman should be stripped of his Nobel Prize (which comes from dirty money resulting from the less than noble Nobel family funds gained through the manufacture of gunpowder—hardly a liberal icon).

But we should give him a new prize—The Clinton Prize— for crony and criminal capitalism.

This *haut* arrogant intellectual of modest origins, whose family escaped the pogroms of Belarus in the last century, has grossly misled the modern American public for decades. He is disconnected from the everyman. He has failed to tell the truth about his *dogma* of globalism. A thin-skinned Panglossian, he is the very source of American demise.

It's time the New York crowd stopped giving him credit and instead called him what he is: *Wrong.*

4

THE CONTEXT

THE RISE OF NATIONALISM CAN NO LONGER BE DENIED

June 23, 2016, will go down in British history as a most significant date—rivaling VE Day, the fall of the Berlin Wall, and even the Battle of Hastings in 1066. The vote to leave the EU is that important!

Like our own Fourth of July, June 23 will forevermore become known as Independence Day.

This breaking news story appears shocking to many, but is good for Donald Trump. And it rounds out a very bad week for President Obama and Hillary Clinton—Brexit plus the Supreme Court decision on immigration. Take note: the rise of nationalism can no longer be denied. It is a growing phenomenon not to be dismissed or ignored.

The British people in a democratic action have made their

voice known and voted to leave the European Union. Article 50 of the Treaty of Lisbon will now be invoked, and Great Britain will no longer be tied to the yoke of Brussels. It will no longer have to foot the excessive bill presented by the Eurocrats or follow their dictates.

The euroskeptics, led by the likes of likely future Prime Minister Boris Johnson and cabinet members such as Michael Gove, Iain Duncan Smith, and Priti Patel, have won the day and prevailed. As the queen herself purportedly said, "Give me three good reasons for staying in Europe." The prime minister has announced he will step down by October, as he was utterly defeated.

The Union Jack can fly high again.

This does not mean the British won't buy German cars, drink French wine, employ Polish plumbers, or stop eating Italian pasta. What it does mean is that it will no longer give rise or be party to a European superstate that is controlled outside its national boundaries and its legally defined sovereignty.

Freedom was the rallying cry, and in a 52 to 48 percent victory (with over 72 percent turnout) the British people have accomplished what was thought impossible and unlikely only a few months ago. The argument for "taking your country back" won out over the fear mongering of David Cameron (Conservative leader), Jeremy Corbyn (Labour leader), and Tim Farron (Liberal leader)—and the entire British establishment. The elites have lost!

The vote broke into interesting regional differences with London and the South and Scotland voting to Remain, while the rest of England voted overwhelmingly to leave.

Make no mistake, this is a popular revolution; it is nothing less. One question it raises worldwide is this: Is the reaction against globalism the new political tidal wave, and does it signal an eventual Trump presidency?

The effect on the British pound and on global markets is already being felt with massive selloffs and hits to the value of sterling. These are not thought to be lasting. Stabilization will prevail. But it will be a volatile period as the world adjusts to newfound populism and as the rest of Europe comes to terms with the great divorce. Indeed, a number of other European countries, from the Netherlands to Denmark to possibly France, may in time hold their own referendums, and the European project in the form of Brusselsocracy could be shattered and taken down—brick by brick.

When all is said and done there are four major conclusions to draw from the historic Brexit vote. They have to do with liberty, security, economy, and global relations.

Taking up the cause of Locke and casting aside the philosophy of the European Rousseau, the Brits have cemented their place on the side of liberty. The Anglo-Saxon rule of law and the democratic spirit of a free people have triumphed over statism and the centralization of power.

The security of Britain was paramount in the campaign, and the notion that they would not be able to control their own borders clearly struck home. The immigration issue and the absolute fear of tides of people flowing into the country unabated gave rise to much of the populist and nationalist sentiment. The very posters used depicted throngs of masses in line to enter from outside the EU. A picture tells a thousand words, as the slogan goes. Britain also rejected the EU call for a standing army, instead wanting to double down on NATO, which has served it and the West so well.

The economic consequence of leaving Europe weighed heavily in the debate, and nearly every economist, all the banks, and most of the large companies put forth a case that the economic costs of departure would be great. They lost.

The people wanted democracy more than a loaf of bread or more cash into the pockets of the "wankers"—as the super-rich are known here in the United Kingdom. The cost of staying in Europe was actually equally great, and this case won the day. Loathing the unelected European institutions and their high expense and undemocratic nature has proved untenable for the UK, at least.

Britain's place in the world is well established both historically, in the Commonwealth, and in terms of size and role. Did tying its cart to a struggling and desperate union of twenty-eight very different European partners make any sense? The answer was "No."

Britain never joined the Euro currency or the European Central Bank, so the decision to leave all the other trappings of a failing Europe should not be made out to be more than it is. Britain is and will always be an island nation, apart from the continent and part of a "special relationship" with its distant cousin and former colony, the only superpower, the United States of America.

After the historic Brexit vote, this "special relationship" should be reassessed as the future of liberty depends on it. It is proper to ask: Will it survive the rest of this twenty-first century? Is it now perhaps more important than ever?

Our mutual and abiding interests, common worldview, congruence of sympathies, and the undeniably unique heritage of the Anglo-American tradition of *liberty* should be our true future together. In my view with a shared Whig history, the King James Bible, the Anglican Church, long historical memory—all of these things make up a valuable Anglo-Atlanticist patrimony. Britain and America belong together, not in Europe.

The future will need such Anglo-American leadership more than ever before. Perhaps, herein lie the true "sinews of lasting peace," as Churchill himself phrased it.

But the words that ring today throughout Britain, chiming from steeples and sung by loud choristers—in every town and in every Hobbit-like shire are those of the past civil-rights leader, "Free at last, free at last, Thank God almighty, we are free at last."

REVENGE OF THE LITERATI

The literati (otherwise known as intellectuals, most of whom occupy positions in academe) are a self-conscious special class. Their communication skills can at times make them valuable but also troublesome members of their respective societies. In developed and developing countries, they become problematic when they begin to consider themselves the *high priests* of their respective societies—namely, the arbiters of fundamental values, or worse still, they try to assume political office in a kind of "academocracy."

In the United States, the literati take two forms: conservative and liberal. Both seek revenge.

The former, namely the conservatives (e.g., those running the *National Review*, *Wall Street Journal*, etc.), are typically secularists willing to tolerate traditional centers of cultural authority such as religion and the family as long as those centers adhere to the secular catechism as defined by themselves: (1) There is a collective good vouchsafed to the conservative literati (their version of substituting politics for religion or taming religion to fit their politics); (2) Ivy-league speech and writing norms; (3) globalism; (4) dogmatic commitment to free markets, and (5) universal representative democracy (the neocons prefer interventionist nation-building abroad).

These ideologue conservatives and neocons dislike Donald Trump because he violates their basic five commandments. Since in the minds of the conservative literati these commandments are beyond reproach and therefore beyond debate, they refuse to engage Trump in a discussion that would require opening up these commandments for honest and full review.

From the point of view of the conservative literati, Trump takes no "substantive" positions (i.e., he does not endorse or exemplify their basic commandments without reservation; and when he outlines policy stances they do not form a neat deductive system as required by academic logic). Hence, any discussion of Trump degenerates quickly into either character assassination or speculation on his hidden private ambitions and egoism or, worse, an alleged authoritarianism.

These conservatives' attitude and dogma were perfectly demonstrated recently by Bret Stephens, the deputy editorial page editor for the *Wall Street Journal* when he told CNN: "I most certainly will not vote for Donald Trump. I will vote for the least left-wing opponent to Donald Trump, and I want to make a vote to make sure that he has—that he is the biggest loser in presidential history since, I don't know, Alf Landon or going back further."

Said Stephens, "It's important that Donald Trump and what he represents—this kind of ethnic, quote, 'conservatism,' or populism—be so decisively rebuked that the Republican Party, the Republican voters, will forever learn their lesson that they cannot nominate a man so manifestly unqualified to be president in any way, shape or form."

The liberal literati follow a remarkably similar pattern, as demonstrated by the *New York Times, Atlantic, New Yorker*, PBS, and most of the media. But, they are dedicated secular humanists unwilling to tolerate Judeo-Christian institutions. (Islam is fine because it is a temporary stick with which to beat the other forms of monotheism.)

The radical secular-humanist catechism includes: (1) There

is a collective good vouchsafed exclusively to the liberal literati (their version of substituting politics for religion); (2) Ivy-league speech and writing norms; (3) globalism; (4) the basic innate goodness of all human beings (this is why it is so important to reject any Christian concept of sin); (5) evil is the result of environmental determinism (called victimization); (6) the existence of a social technology vouchsafed to social scientists at major universities; (7) the need for an all-powerful government, perhaps in time, a world government, to employ that social technology as administered by their expert graduates; and (8) redistributionist democratic-socialism when properly informed by the all-knowing liberal literati.

The liberal literati exhibit two current forms of behavior: sharp hatred of Trump and loving forgiveness of the Clintons.

They dislike Trump because he violates all of their basic commandments. Since in the minds of the liberal literati these commandments are beyond reproach and therefore beyond debate, they refuse to engage Trump in a discussion that would require opening up these commandments for review and inspection.

From the point of view of the liberal literati, Trump takes no "substantive" positions (i.e., he does not endorse or exemplify their basic commandments; and when he outlines policy stances they do not form a neat deductive system as required by their liberal academic orthodoxy and logic). Hence, any discussion of Trump degenerates into vicious character assassination and hatred or even accusations of fascism. That fear is always lurching behind their façade of openness. Name-calling is easier than debate.

With regard to Hillary: She is seen as an intellectual genius

(Yale Law School but a "mute inglorious Milton" because her commitment never gave her sufficient time to write anything memorable); courageous in character (consciously willing to take whatever heat Fox News generates about her systematic lying when that lying is in the service of the 'cause'); selfless devotion to all minorities (willing to vote for the Democratic Party and diversity, quotas and any form of statism—from health care to welfare/free goods); martyr for women's liberation, willing to spend a lifetime loyally married to a known predator and abuser (who no doubt was himself somehow a victim); and a foreign-policy wonder-star (all of whose failed or botched policies were sabotaged by the military, the FBI and the CIA).

Case closed!

Oh to rediscover the ancient and Christian account of true intellectual life without revenge. St. Augustine in his "On Free Will," described it as "an effort to gather our whole soul ... to station ourselves and become wholly entrenched ... so that we may no longer rejoice in our own private goods, which are bound up with ephemeral things, but instead cast aside all attachment to times and places and apprehend that which is always one and the same."

Forget the literati—not in an anti-intellectual tradition but realizing that a vote for Trump and such eternal thought may again be possible, if he also defunds higher education and calls the literati on both sides what they are: merely ideologues.

WHO'S SPEWING "HATE SPEECH"?

Last week, I spoke at a purportedly evangelical Christian college in Vancouver, Canada, where I encountered, to my utter and complete surprise, the worst forms of hate.

Knowing I had written columns supporting Donald Trump, the faculty and some students protested my speaking and lambasted my lecture.

This was despite my efforts to write the editorials supporting Trump from a moderate and reasoned perspective. Perhaps my mistake was to think that my writing could persuade by suggesting the need for a more inclusive and less elitist political process.

The topic for the lecture at Regent College addressed the question of how we can go about building good, ethical corporations. My focus, I believed, was about morals, values and culture—*not* about politics, although that is how the protesting faculty and students chose to interpret my purpose in being there, as well as the lecture content I delivered.

On the day of my lecture, the college newspaper, named *&c* whatever that means, had a front-page article attacking my speech and views.

The article read as follows:

> We imagine some of you are astonished by the political debacle taking place to your south. Donald Trump, whose electrifying demagoguery has garnered a frenzy of support from people—many of whom are professing Christians—in the USA appalls us.

Like some notorious politicians and dictators before him, Donald Trump had galvanized his followers by playing to people's fears and channeling their anger toward easy targets like ethnic minorities and immigrants, whom he, among other things, accuses of taking American jobs.

Put simply, Trump, playing the strong man, is providing scapegoats to people who want someone to blame for personal and societal disappointments, and they love him for it.

In everything he is doing, he is fueling the narrative that we live in a dog-eat-dog world and that he is the alpha dog that can ensure that his constituents have enough. Trump's self-aggrandizing power is idolatrous: it depends upon the denigration of the powerless. He is robing himself in falsehood to appear as one with authority, but ultimately, this emperor has no clothes.

Now, I was treated rudely, disregarded and accused of hate—but let's unpack the rhetoric in this logic a bit to see who the real haters are.

The idea that my editorials on Trump might be fairly argued and moderately written appears to be antithetical to the far-left Bernie socialists, including former weathermen and now the overtly aggressive Black Lives Matter radicals who populate today's protest marches, mixed together with anarchists from the Occupy movements, as well as those being paid by wealthy socialist forces like Soros to disrupt free speech and cause harm to the very fabric of civility.

First, be clear, Christians are overwhelmingly supporting Trump in spite of his many shortcomings because they see what has happened to the spiritual capital in America, a country they love.

This is why Trump has consistently won the vast majority of the evangelical votes in every single state. Personalities like Jerry Falwell Jr., Rev. Robert Jeffress, and Mike Huckabee, among others, have endorsed Trump.

What the student and faculty slamming my presence on campus fail to realize is that the radical far left has worked for decades to obliterate any semblance of Christian values in an America the far left desperately wants to secularize.

Second, Americans are angry and have a right to be so, just as Christ upset the tables in the Temple in Jerusalem run by the moneychangers.

The political elite, along with the mainstream media increasingly controlled by the far left has disabused American middle-class citizens for too long.

Trump supporters see him as a Washington outsider who has not built his career as a professional politician.

Trump supporters agree America is not a sovereign nation as long as the southern border with Mexico is left open and largely unguarded.

This is why in the United States we have 12 million illegal immigrants and more on the way, not to mention a drug war.

Would Canada allow such a travesty?

Third, a majority of Americans may end up voting for Trump because he represents placing traditional American values above interest-group politics and crony capitalism.

Trump might also be right that globalists have stacked a free-trade world economy in favor of multinational corporate profits, at the expense of exploiting low-cost labor and exploiting natural resources anywhere and everywhere either can be found.

In the face of free-trade globalism, Trump has made it clear he intends to defend the national interest to bring jobs back by negotiating better trade deals—a formula Trump believes has the best chance of ensuring American prosperity.

Isn't that what Americans expect of a leader?

Is it authoritarian or hateful to suggest and enforce real policies, or is it the responsibility of a leader who truly wants to serve his people?

In the great tradition of Western civilization, the notion of a servant leader, expressed in Christ, is a model to follow and uphold not decry.

Lastly, aside from all the trite language in the editorial that parades as a front-page news article in the Vancouver college newspaper, Trump is no emperor.

Trump may better be portrayed as a gladiator in the arena who will fight for the common person, who will defend freedom, who will build and rebuild American infrastructure and who will in his own theme: Make America Great Again.

Is this unappealing to Canadians and others who for decades have depended on American largesse, on our military shield, on our nuclear deterrence, on our charity, on our economic engine of growth?

Or does the world prefer a weak America, rudderless in a multi-polar world, possibly led by a spineless world government?

Trump is no hater, and it is wrong to assume all Trump supporters are haters.

What do Trump supporters want? The answer involves the restoration and perpetuation of America as "a city on a hill."

Trump supporters want America to be the beacon and light it once was.

Trump supporters want America to be respected once again.

Increasingly, this election is all about freedom—not about the hate we are hearing today from business and political leaders, pastors, university faculty and students who appear to hate Trump as much as they hate the idea of a traditionally moral Christian America dedicated, as our Founding Fathers understood, to Christian morals that supported profitable business founded with an understanding of spiritual capital.

THE DEATH OF EUROPE

I readily admit to being a Eurocentric Europhile.

Please bear with me as I detail some personal history to establish the background for why I make this statement.

- My family roots are in Scotland, Holland, and Germany, and my entire education, faith, and upbringing, while quintessentially American, are deeply rooted in the European experience. My faith is founded in the Protestant Reformation that shook Europe five hundred years ago.

- I spent nine formative summers teaching and touring throughout all of Europe while I was in graduate school and as a young professor.

- I still recall with wild enthusiasm my first trip to Europe in 1972 at age nineteen. I studied and took degrees and have lectured at European universities. I was a Deutches Austauschendienst at Kiel Universitat and was made an honorary member of the Christian Democratic Party of the Netherlands as early as 1979.

- I was president of the four ancient Scottish universities trusts in the United States. I wrote a doctoral dissertation largely about European ideas—in politics, philosophy, and economics.

- I lived four years in Geneva, Switzerland, in an ambassadorial post in the United Nations in the late '80s until 1992 when European history shifted and the Cold War ended.

I had a front-row seat as deputy executive secretary of the UN Economic Commission for Europe. I was an executive board member of the World Economic Forum, which started as the European Management Forum for CEOs.

- I was actually present at the Berlin Wall just days after it came down. My friends in Eastern Europe, the radical economists, all became leading figures—ministers, central bankers, and prime ministers in their respective countries after the fall of the Soviet Union.

- I was an adviser to the Polish government during its shock therapy and privatization. I speak several European languages, regularly read European books, magazines and newspapers, and have been a firm supporter of the so-called Atlantic Alliance my entire life.

To steal a line from President Kennedy, "*Ich bin ein Europaisch.*"

So, it is with a deep sense of disappointment and true sadness that I have to say what I am about to say.

ADRIFT WITHOUT A SOUL

Europe's churches are empty. Mass on Sundays, in any Gothic cathedral, is virtually unattended, except for a handful of tourists, vacant. The actual celebration of Mass is typically conducted in a side chapel, fit for the dozen or so worshipers who show up for service.

Europe is adrift without a soul and evolving rapidly away from its moorings.

In his book, *The Cube and the Cathedral*, George Weigel

described a European culture that has become not only increasingly secular but in many cases downright hostile to Christianity.

The cathedral in his title is Notre Dame, now overshadowed in cultural importance by the Arc de la Defense, the ultra modernist "cube" that dominates an office complex outside Paris.

"European man has convinced himself that in order to be modern and free, he must be radically secular," Weigel writes. "That conviction and its public consequences are at the root of Europe's contemporary crisis of civilizational morale."

Recall the rancorous debate over whether or not "Christianity" should be explicitly acknowledged when drafting the European Union's constitutional treaty.

By the time the draft constitution was completed, a grudging reference to "the cultural, religious, and humanist inheritance of Europe" had been shoehorned into the preamble's first clause. This was about as much religion as Europe could stomach in a constitution that runs some seventy thousand words.

Practicing Christianity in Europe today enjoys a status not dissimilar to closet status reserved for smoking marijuana or engaging in unorthodox sexual activities decades ago. Few Europeans will mind if you do so in private, but please have the courtesy to keep the matter private.

Today, Christianity in the EU is considered at best a retrograde and largely atavistic practice barely tolerated in a self-described "progressive" society devoted to obtaining the good material life, including long holidays, short work hours and generous government benefits.

Dare we ask what is the deeper source of European antipathy to religion?

The problem goes all the way back to the fourteenth

century, when scholastics like William of Ockham argued for "nominalism." According to their philosophy, universals—concepts such as "justice" or "freedom" and qualities such as "good"—do not exist in the abstract but are merely words that denote instances of what they describe. A current of thought was set into motion, Weigel among others believes, that pulled European man away from transcendent truths. One casualty was any fixed idea of human nature.

If there is no such thing as human nature, then there are no universal moral principles that can be read from human nature. If there are no universal moral truths, then religion positing them is merely a form of oppression or myth, one from which Europe's elites see themselves as now liberated. And they look down on their American and Third World cousins who continue to believe in such irrational flights of fancy.

I think the critics are on firm ground when they analyze Europe's present condition, with its low birth rates, heavy government debts, Muslim immigration worries and tendency to carp from the sidelines when the fate of nations is at stake. Like Weigel, one could sketch the worst-case scenario—the "bitter end"—for a Europe that is religiously bereft, demographically moribund and morally without a compass: "The muezzin summons the faithful to prayer from the central loggia of St. Peter's in Rome, while Notre-Dame has been transformed into Hagia Sophia on the Seine—a great Christian church become an Islamic museum."

One need not find this scenario altogether plausible to feel persuaded by more measured arguments about Europe's atheistic humanism. Without a religious dimension, a commitment to human freedom is likely to be attenuated, too weak to make sacrifices in its name. Europe's political elites especially, but its citizens as well, believe in freedom and democracy, of course, but they are reluctant to put the "good life" on hold and put lives on the line when freedom is in need of a champion—in the Balkans, the Sudan, Darfur or in Iraq cum Syria.

The good of human freedom, by European lights, must be weighed against the risk and cost of actually fighting for it. It is no longer transcendent, absolute. In such a world, governed by a narrow utilitarian calculus, sacrifice is rare, churches go unattended, and over time the spiritual capital that brought forth all that we know as the West is at risk of being lost.

Europe is a society adrift, untied from the source of its greatness—the very cultural foundation that provided the values making Europe great is disintegrating, leaving Europe (and soon the entire West) on sinking sand. More specifically, as the past is erased, re-written, or ignored, the rich Judeo-Christian history of Europe is being left behind.

And at what cost?

As I ponder this thesis, I am reminded of Orwell's quote, "We have now sunk to a depth at which restatement of the obvious is the first duty of intelligent men." It is obvious, "culture determines civilization." Without its distinctly Christian history, Europe would not be what it is.

Unfortunately, we may now have more accurately to write, "Europe would not have been what it was."

America is now alone in defending freedom and upholding the tradition of faith and reason. Trump is our defender.

WHY RELIGIOUS LIBERTY IS
KEY TO PROSPERITY

Freedom of religion and economic freedom actually go together like—well, you fill in the blank. One is not possible without the other because they emanate from the same source. They not only gravitate in a similar and related direction, but they originate from the same basic truths and are two sides of the same coin.

We are increasingly finding in the twenty-first century that nations and economies that witness religious liberty have greater economic freedom, and that countries with the most economic freedom also engender more religious liberty and democracy. The reason for this can be summed up in a single word, and that word is "competition."

Freedom of religion in the Western tradition and evidenced in Western nation-states is generally considered to be a fundamental right. As such, it is underscored by a guarantee of respective sovereign governments to allow the freedom of belief for individuals, including women and children, as well as the freedom of worship for all persons and groups. Logically, freedom of religion also includes the freedom not to follow any religion at all.

In the last three decades, the concept of economic freedom has grown out of the writings of notable, mostly neo-classical economists. The agreed cornerstones of economic freedom are: personal choice rather than collective action; voluntary exchange coordinated by markets rather than allocation via the political process; freedom to enter and compete in markets; and protection of persons and their property from aggression or harm by others.

While there is much debate on which precise policies promote economic freedom most, there is more or less agreement that the size, expenditures and taxes of government and the right to enterprise formation along with the legal structure and security of property rights are most essential to its flourishing. Access to sound money and transparent capital markets, freedom to trade internationally and minimal regulation of credit, labor and business also count a great deal.

The nation-states/economies with the most economic freedom witness individuals that are free to work, produce, consume, and invest in the way they please, and their freedom is both protected by the state and unconstrained by it. In locations of economic freedom that can be measured and scaled, there are free public and private companies, in other words, enterprises that flourish as a result of the protection of both the rule of law and enforced codes of business. Business law and capital market access are twin pillars that allow entrepreneurs the freedom to start businesses, merge businesses, and sell businesses in freedom and without political interference or undue regulation.

The corollary, namely that religious liberty begets economic freedom, is now provable. If we desire more economic freedom, we need to begin by insuring religious liberty. If we want economic growth and development, we need to tolerate and permit religious groups and persons to do as they choose.

Competition for religious activity is as healthy as for economic activity.

Those states that fail to allow economic freedom are universally those that do not permit religious liberty. And likewise, those that fail to encourage religious liberty almost always, it turns out, fail to give rise to economies of prosperity with economic freedom. Some countries may have mineral or other wealth or large productive workforces, but they cannot sustain their economic growth. Why? It circles back to the link between religious and economic freedom.

"Spiritual capital" is the missing link.

In the same way money capital accumulates in savings accounts, spiritual capital is built up over time through habits of the heart, realized in mediating structures, such as families, churches and religious institutions, social groups, schools and in the wider culture. Here is a truism that has become more apparent as secularization theories and modernization models have fallen by the wayside or been overcome or contradicted by factual reality: Religious freedom gives rise to economic freedom and the formation of every kind of capital, including spiritual capital.

In the twenty-first century, the abiding questions for a more integrated global economy remains these: Does your religious liberty match your economic freedom and vice versa? If not, why not? And if so, how so?

The analysis of new comprehensive data demonstrates that the countries with the least religious liberty also suffer the worst economic freedoms and are lacking in political rights. Who are they? Let's name names: Burma, China-Tibet, Eritrea, Iran, Iraq, Maldives, North Korea, Saudi Arabia, Sudan, Turkmenistan and Uzbekistan come in as the worst of the worst. But following not far behind are Afghanistan, Bangladesh, Belarus, China, Cuba, Mauritania, Pakistan, Palestine, and Vietnam.

When you look at religious freedom and economic freedom

in comparison to ratings of civil liberties, a number of countries pop out as especially problematic and include: Bangladesh, India, Maldives, Serbia, Kosovo, and Turkey.

Countries or economies that dwell in the never-ending cycle of poverty are often those with the least freedom of religion or economy.

As totalitarian regimes or kleptocracies, they are too often either cults of personality built around the leader of the opportune moment, or a defunct ideology. Some are desperate places that still exhibit tribalism and internecine warfare. Others have come to live like welfare queens dependent upon guilt-ridden developed countries that are quick to give aid but slow to build or invest.

The mistake is trying to separate things that are forever joined, that naturally go together.

Linking religious liberty to economic freedom is the key to developing robust economic activity capable of generating prosperity. This is why linking religious liberty to economic freedom must become the clarion call of humane people and enlightened nations today seeking to form enterprises of lasting value, in every country, every region, and on every continent.

THE FORGOTTEN WHITE AMERICAN MALE

Women, minorities, and other marginalized groups have multiple champions.

Picture right now in your mind's eye: Hillary, Ellen DeGeneres, Elton John, Black Lives Matter, hey, even the redone, Caitlyn Jenner.

No one has spoken for white males in a *very* long time it seems.

Frankly, it's been taboo to do so. If you did, you'd be called misogynistic, sexist, racist, homophobic, whatever. That's part of why Trump's campaign took off like a rocket—he crossed over the lines of political correctness. Can we at least raise the issue? Well in a closet, perhaps?

What we need finally, is a *champion* who will not back down in the face of progressive opposition—or any other kind of hate speech or disrespect and begin to speak for men. Did I just say that? It was very balsy of me.

This is what lies underneath the populist phenomenon. The "smart people" are telling themselves that we are going through a post-industrial revolution. Yeah, yeah … Men had to come off the farms, into the mines and factories. Now they have to come out of the factories into the cubicles. But that's far from the whole story and Donald J. Trump knows it.

There's plenty of industry going on around the world—just less and less of it in the United States these days and in the savaged rustbelt. We have chosen to extend privileges to capital that maintains a small, and getting smaller, strata of managers (call them bosses) at extraordinary income levels, while outsourcing our manufacturing to poorer nations.

And what happened to our manhood? What happened when little Marco challenged the size of The Donald's hands? Yes, with the candidacy of Trump *manhood* came back into focus.

Even that is only part of the much, much larger story. Males are statistically doing less well in school these days. Boys are seen as bad. Men live shorter lives. They die early and they even shoot each other. Lower middle class communities have been decimated by the combined forces of the never-ending sexual revolution and by enduring economic stagnation. Charles Murray documented all this in his frightening sociological tome, *Coming Apart*.

The white men who occupy boardrooms do not give a flying f* about this saga and travail as long as they and their progeny remain in control of finance and *all* the elite institutions. Why should they?

But will their sons become men?

Do you remember James Dean's line in the 1955 classic film, *Rebel Without a Cause?*

I know that dates me but it is a *classic*, no?

He asked his father this telling question, "What do you do when you have to be a man?"

His father didn't know. Worse still, he had no clue. There were no guidelines to follow, no rules to master, no script to read. Hell, there were no profound answers to that question.

That is the dilemma we face today. We don't know or have forgotten about manliness.

Now I am no crazy, deep, backwoodsman, drum-beating warrior type, who wants us to go native or primitive. I don't wear a loincloth or kill my own dinner (I do shoot ducks and pheasant occasionally).

I just think we need to get back to basics about manhood.

We need to figure this out or we will be (are *already* being) replaced. A woman can go to the doctor and get fertilized by donor sperm and never see a man, have a husband, or have sex. God forbid they have sons—as they would have no role models. Is that the future?

So using a technique that is used in the intelligence world (yes, spy-dom), in the military and in corporate life, I want to suggest *four* scenarios on the future on manhood.

More proverbially, I want to ask: *Who's your Daddy*—in the year let's say, arbitrarily, 2025? That's far enough off that we can't really know but it is not too far off that we don't care.

So get out a piece of paper for me and let's do an exercise in *futures thinking*.

Think of it as strategic planning to consider the longer term. Foresight, if you like, through more than one lens. It entails using a macro-scope, instead of a microscope.

You don't have a macro-scope? Just pretend.

On one side (axis) of your paper, write down **strong** and along the other axis insert **weak**. Got it: strong vs. weak. Easy . . . you are a born futurist.

I get paid a lot of money for this kind of heady stuff, so don't laugh.

There are four boxes on your paper, right?

Can you see them?

The header is **Manhood**. Write it down.

MANHOOD

Superman	Metrosexual
Father Knows Best	Girlie-Man

Lower left box, let's call that strong/weak, or *Father Knows Best*. It was a great TV series that I grew up on and it is the standard, old fashion view of manhood.

Let's inspect and list its characteristics.

This middle class, probably mid-western and traditional values/family man is good, humble, but all knowing. And he is the head of the house, which is after all his castle. He is firm but fair, decisive and modestly aggressive. As a man he knows both his own place and is responsible for his kinship band—the nuclear/extended family. The man is pragmatic but principled and self-aware. He is faithfully monogamous and unambiguous about his manliness. He is comfortable in his own skin and believes in power and tradition *both*.

Second Box upper left, is super strong or better, Superman. What are its characteristics?

As a superhero, rooted in comic book fame, there is a fictional side to this man. Since he was born on the planet *Krypton* and raised in America as Clark Kent, there is something quite unreal about him. With super born - human abilities, he not only wears a red cape with the letter 'S' emblazoned but is capable of deeds larger than life. Hyper-able and athletic, this man is influenced by Nietzsche's concept of Ubermensch. He dominates woman and is promiscuous. Super rough and overly aggressive, supermen attack and terrorize wrongdoers and all gangsters, as only a ruthless vigilante would do. Superman actually comes in two flavors: good and bad.

Lower right quadrant is weak, call it, Girlie-man.

What are its characteristics? Make a list.

Although used by then Governor Arnold Schwarzenegger pejoratively, after seeing an SNL skit on the bodybuilders Hans and Franz, these men commit the horror of insulting gay men. This ironic mockery has become ensconced as more than a comic façade. A girlie-man is effeminate, primped up, and weak even when showing an outward appearance of strength. There is a fake understanding about sexuality and a weakness that becomes an overriding feature both physically and emotionally. They are like girls in many ways.

Last Box is upper far right, super strong and super weak, and a kind of combo man we could name, Metrosexual.

What are its characteristics?

This is the perfectly androgynous male who is neither from Venus or Mars. He is urban, enjoys shopping oh so much, is into fashion, and possesses traits normally associated with women or homosexual men. They can't walk past a Banana Republic store without making a purchase. They use moisturizer. Their ringtones come from Kimpossible. In their fitted jeans, with plucked unibrows and perfectly groomed hair, these men are the ultimate consumers and exhibit narcissist qualities. Neither straight nor gay, they have all of the characteristics of gays and the dress. For them it is "all about breaking gender roles."

Now, looking at these four archetypes in the year 2025—of manhood—where would you place yourself? Where would you like to see men down the road? Where is America going long-term? Where do you think your sons will be? Your grand-sons? What do you think is most likely given the present trend line? Is this evolving? Set in stone? Reversible? And what are the implications?

Here's the *takeaway*. Manliness or traditional masculinity, i.e., being courageous, direct, and assertive, as the true authority on a subject, is dying off. Harvard political philosopher Harvey Mansfield Jr. suggested as much in his controversial book *Manliness*.

The word *virility*, a synonym of *manliness*, is no longer even used. The notion that there is an etiquette wherein a man respects himself and earns the respect of others has surely dissipated.

Name me a definitive act of valor you have witnessed recently. Is there such a thing as self-sacrifice any longer in the "me generation"? And the old fashion idea that we are here to *serve* others has flown away. Selfishness is the norm and the expectation nowadays. But these other, older values used to be the themes of true manhood. In fact, General George Patton, who was no wuss, wrote a little booklet based on them and gave them to all our troops during WW II. He wanted real men on the front line. He wanted to win against those fascists. He knew that men needed to be taught the basics of manhood.

He could have said since the time of ancient Homer the ideas of chivalry and confident assertiveness have been the *eternal* inspiration, the very image and inspiration of the race. He could have recounted the creation story (Adam and Eve *not* Adam and Steve) or the legacy of the entire history of mankind.

We still have some remote but fading remembrance of the days of chivalry, where men showed courtesy to women and children, where they were gentle benefactors to their communities, hence the word *gentlemen*. These knights of yore saw the responsibility of manhood as a noble *calling*—it had theological bearing as well as a long-standing tradition.

All that is gone. The history of manhood if it were to be written would likely start with some distant, unrecognizable warrior-like stories about a caste of men in battle and at war. War is part of warrior, sorry. But where would it end?

By the time of early America after our independence this tale evolved into one about yeoman farmers and then artisans. The industrial revolution changed all that. Men moved off the farm and into the factories. There they still made things (well, until recent decades) but they no longer had economic independence. They were workers for someone else. The notion of being a "breadwinner" prevailed but manhood was slowly emasculated,the definition of which is to deprive a man of his male identity. Privilege was stripped away and attacked; even their very manhood was questioned or abbreviated. Should we add neutered?

Today, which of the *four* scenarios best describes reality? And where is it honestly headed by 2025?

We have a crisis of manhood today. Ponder those four scenarios we just created about the future again, and ask James Dean's profound question all over again.

Should we cling to the past? Recreate some new age version of man? Redefine manliness? Or should we just bid it farewell and good riddance forever and accept some new form of androgyny?

Is there a normative concept of manliness that works across time, place, and culture—or is that too much to ask? Is manliness still a virtue? Are there *any* virtues at all in a skeptical and relativistic age?

For Aristotle and the ancients, if we care to look back, it was a grave and perennial concern. It meant being all you can be. (The US Army stole his concept for their slogan.) It was tied up with *excellence.* He called it "human flourishing." *Virtu* itself meant masculine strength in Latin. It was conceived as the opposite of womanhood and developmentally the graduation from childhood.

Today, we are incapable of making these distinctions. We are lost—without a guide, a Bible, or a reliable compass.

The best we can come up with is some phony Five Male Traits from a web search. Yes, there are websites on "muscle for life." They advertise the benefits of caffeinated energy drinks for men as well as herbal supplements (let your imagination run loose) for other organs.

And those five masculine traits are?

- *Don't aim for ease.* I like this because it sounds like TR and his emphasis on the "strenuous life."

- *See the world as it is.* A dose of realism never hurt. It could have added: and make the most of it, quoting John Wayne, who is after all a picture of cowboy manliness.

- *Never complain or make excuse.* Stiff upper lip is very British and Churchillian, I suppose. Real men are not crybabies.

- *Never quit.* A bit redundant but who likes a quitter or a loser for that matter?

- *Never pity anyone.*

In our networked world and socially minded age of discovered consciousness, right mindfulness and near total and
constant social media, I should leave you with this resource in
case you are dumfounded or need a context or want to pick
a scenario to execute for yourself and live it out. Trump is
reminding Americans daily of the lost definition of manliness.

Try: *wikihow.com/Be-man*ly. It even comes with pictures.

5

TRUMP'S POLICIES

TRUMP'S PATH TO FIXING TRADE

Presumptive president Donald Trump's *new* trade policy should focus on these key elements, if it is to succeed at the overarching thematic of his presidency, namely, Making America Great Again.

Trump is a free trader by instinct, and as he has stated he has no plan to return to the failed Smoot-Hawley plan of the 1930s, rest assured.

The economic reality is that tariffs usually don't work. Countries retaliate, and all parties lose in a trade war. So what *realistically* can be done by Trump on trade?

On the *supply side*, the United States must *constantly* get more competitive.

This includes more research and development, constant innovation, advanced technological manufacturing, improved access to capital, renewed skills training and benchmarking. A pro-growth environment, if earnestly followed by Trump, will lead to prosperity and rising standards of living and increased wages for *all* Americans.

On the *demand side*, first, Trump should cool off on all the Obama trade deals. Put them on hold or ice. The Trans-Pacific Parternship, struck with eleven Asian countries, is a bad deal. Has anyone read all fifty-six hundred pages of it? The one with the EU is no better.

Next, confront China on its currency manipulation.

This is rarely discussed but is at the heart of our trade imbalance. The Treasury Department biannual report to Congress on exchange-rate practices of our trading partners confirms Trump's analysis—that foreign countries are eating our lunch and that the US government is doing little or nothing about it. Under current procedures, by the time we finish pleading with them to halt their unfair practices, there will be little or no industrial economy left in this country.

Under enhanced reporting criteria set forth by Congress in the Trade Enhancement and Trade Facilitation Act of 2015, Treasury names five countries—China, Japan, Korea, Taiwan, and Germany—whose trade policies pose a threat to the United States and global economies.

This is nothing more than a "name and shame" document since each of the countries only meets two of the three necessary criteria for (ineffective) action. Thus all Treasury does is put the countries on a new "monitoring" list. That means we watch them while they continue to steal factories and jobs from the United States. And, even if the countries did meet all three criteria, the weak potential penalties are rather toothless—and can be reversed by the president basically at will.

We need a concrete plan that fixes this with *immediate action*.

Currency misdealing can no longer be tolerated. If need be, we can play the same game.

Make no mistake, China and other countries also routinely break the rules by dumping their products below cost in the US market. Some also specialize in making counterfeit products, thereby costing the companies who make the authentic products over $20 billion a year.

Trump needs to tell China, and any other nation manufacturing fraudulent products, we will add up that bill and assess the tariffs accordingly. They need to police their *own* producers—on their end.

These same countries also use illegal trans-shipping by changing documentation to avoid duties. The penalties on such behavior should be raised a thousand fold. A few shamed examples that are severely penalized would work to end the practice.

It is true Trump will need congressional approval for imposition of any lasting and sizable tariffs on imports. This he can get with a Republican-controlled House and Senate. He does not need approval for short-term, sectoral retaliatory tariffs or negotiations. He can do it himself on Day 1.

Trump can also block US companies from shifting production overseas by taxing them identically at home and abroad, abolishing the foreign tax credit, which avoids double taxation, and by jawboning them, as he has already done with Carrier Corporation, which is planning to move fifteen hundred jobs from Indiana to Mexico. That should set a precedent.

It will be imperative for Trump to work with the Congress as they have jurisdiction over many of these trade matters. With the right vice president, who knows the ins and outs of lawmaking, he will be able quickly to secure all the provisions provided by legislative authority. This should be a top priority.

Honestly, our elites—on both sides of the political spectrum—have been lying about the exaggerated benefits of globalism for decades. It, like free trade, is in reality a mixed bag. Like any equation, there are inevitably winners *and* losers. Unfortunately, the losers have been Americans, and particularly the middle class who work in manufacturing and reside in the Rustbelt.

Free trade, you see, nice as it appears in theory and in economics textbooks, does *not* benefit everyone.

The United States has lost one-third of its jobs over the last fifteen years, over 6 million real workers—gone. And last year the United States ran a $365 billion merchandise trade deficit with China alone, which translates to 2.4 million jobs lost to Chinese imports over the same longer period.

Trump's threat of a 45 percent tariff should be used as what it is—*a threat.* The point is we want reciprocity. Play by the rules, which were set up by the World Trade Organization, or we will react.

This will keep more jobs at home. Open up, or we will close down. That means Japanese car markets, Chinese financial services and access to every other market must change within six months, or we reciprocate and impose on them *exactly* what they impose on us. We have been stupid for far too long, so now, under Trump, we will get smart.

Global trade is not a zero-sum game. Trump must have a comprehensive plan to uphold his promise to the American voters.

This will involve tough negotiations by professionals who know what they are doing and coordination between US Trade Representative and Commerce, Defense, Energy and Treasury, as well as all other government agencies.

Trump should name a trade czar now, who will work for him *alone*—not for any special interests—and who can produce immediate and measurable results.

A new index called the *Trump Prosperity Index* should capture how we are doing, measuring all new jobs created, all jobs returned, economic expansion, the employment participation rate and all trade balances moving in our direction. This one combined number will prove Trump's economic benefits in a telling way.

Trump can produce results and move the needle in the direction it needs to go; the entire country is counting on it, and the result will be a more inclusive capitalism.

UN SKYSCRAPER:

SITE FOR TRUMP'S NEWEST TOWER?

In his book, *Tower of Babble*, a former UN ambassador accused the United Nations of fueling global chaos because of its moral relativism.

Well, how bad is the United Nations?

Donald Trump has said he will send a message to the organization, and it is not going to be one it wants to hear or that it will swallow well. He said in his recent speech to AIPAC, "The United Nations is not a friend of democracy. It's not a friend to freedom."

Only 75 of the 193 members are *real* democracies, according to Freedom House, who ranks such things. They are in for a shock under President Trump, who should cut our payments (25 percent of the whole budget) and drop out of much of what parades as rampant internationalism—and is truly a movement toward one-world government.

Make no mistake, the ideology of the UN is *globalism,* and it has not worked.

With 17 specialized agencies, 14 funds, a secretariat of 18 departments, more than 40,000 overpaid employees, a budget of $5.4 billion a year, peacekeeping missions at $9 billion a year, another $28 billion a year for disaster and development, the UN is by any measure an utter and complete catastrophe.

Most of us have heard about the UN Population Fund, which pays for forced abortions and sterilization, but few know of the UN's far-reaching tentacles—let alone its Human Rights

Commission, which is anti-human rights. The members on that Commission include wonderful and open states like: Algeria, Bolivia, Congo, Cuba, Maldives, Qatar, Russia, Venezuela, and Vietnam.

Now, I know this up close and personal because, during part of the Reagan administration, I had the top UN job in Europe.

Believe me, the UN is a vast and highly politicized bureaucracy with a non-democratic character that is the *most* ineffective of all international organizations. In all honesty, it has had very few real successes since the days of U Thant.

The UN has missed just about every opportunity given to it and especially the more recent ones aimed at reforming itself. It can't stop ethnic cleansing or genocide and certainly has zero effect on Islamic jihadism. It can't glue together failed states, like Syria, or stop bloody wars in places from Rwanda to Sri Lanka.

All attempts to restructure its leadership, finances, infrastructure, and the system itself have had little to no effect.

On the other hand, it has done everything in its power, flying in our face, to establish a Palestinian state in spite of the well-founded allegations of anti-Semitism. Resolution No. 3379 is a case in point, equating Zionism with racism.

And when it comes to scandals, the UN tops the all-time *worst* list. Its Oil for Food Program fiasco, many peacekeeping atrocities, and child sexual abuse scandals, to name but a prominent few, have lead to a near total lack of accountability.

When I was in the UN, many people were on the take, and Mr. 10 Percent, in the form of *kickbacks*, was all over the institution. One fact is certain: Corruption abounds.

So, seventy years on and about half a trillion dollars later, Trump is right to ask: For what?

The UN is bloated, undemocratic, expensive, fragmented and produces few tangible results beyond more platitudes and unattainable left-wing goals. It is a sinecure for aging diplomats and a dumping ground for cronies. And its permanent employees after five years get grandiose tax-free salaries, free education, duty-free alcohol, cigarettes, housing, and petrol. You'd love such a gig, right?

All the audits of the organization turn up the same evidence but *nothing* comes of them. Dag Hammarskjold, the second UN secretary general, once remarked about the UN: "It was created not to lead mankind to heaven but to save humanity from hell."

Trump needs to ask if this is actually true. Or, is the UN instead, a kind of hell on earth? Is it a drag on world peace, and does it resist all suggestions of reform because of its entrenched elites and do-nothing, high-minded, globalist civil servants?

One establishment school of thought keeps saying, if you didn't have the UN, you'd have to invent it. Trump should take up the offer and pronounce the 1945 folly dead on his arrival. Read it its last rites and build a new, vibrant Council of Democracies, more suited to the twenty-first century.

This bipartisan idea, which was backed by Sen. John McCain, among others, suggesting a league of *only* democratic member states that met certain requirements, has its philosophical basis in Kant's notion of "perpetual peace." Autocracies would be excluded, and the new body could provide a very modest multilateral vehicle and end the nonsensical Security Council veto in instances as far ranging as Sudan's Darfur, North Korea or Burma.

Former US ambassador John Bolton was absolutely right when he said, "Quasi-religious faith in engagement and the UN has run into empirical reality. . . . [We should] become more cognizant of that organization's moral and political limitations."

He was being too polite. Trump should sever the chord and stop paying for an anti-American diatribe that does not fulfill its original mission. That tower on East Forty-Second Street in New York City should be put out of business and could be turned into a new Trump edifice with a good water view.

A BETTER OPTION FOR UK:

BECOME OUR FIFTY-FIRST STATE

On June 23 the British people, in a sovereign state called the United Kingdom (consisting of England, Scotland, Wales, and Northern Ireland), vote in a national referendum to decide whether they should remain in the European Union (EU).

What should Americans care?

Sovereignty can be defined in jurisprudence as the full right and power of a governing body to govern itself without *any* interference from outside sources or bodies.

While Brexit is clearly not our choice to make, it appears at least some Americans care a lot—as President Obama spent a few days in London with Prime Minister Cameron lobbying and campaigning hard for the remain vote.

Picture this: A foreign leader intervenes in a sovereign decision of another state. How would Americans feel if some other distant world leader, say, Francois Hollande of France or Robert Mugabe of Zimbabwe, came here to tell us what to do? Really.

Obama said Britain would "go to the back of the queue" (line, in British parlance) in US interests if they did not vote to stay in Europe. He trotted out every argument in the book, also suggesting his globalist Trans-Atlantic Trade and Investment Partnership (TTIP) trade negotiations with Europe would be damaged if the vote were to leave.

Now, there are good reasons *and* bad reasons for and against Brexit, and within the UK the forces are about equally split.

One side, using figures from HM Treasury (albeit a

government agency), suggests it will cost Brits jobs, economic growth, and about $4,000 per head by 2030, if they vote to leave Europe. The calculations have been questioned, and the models seem a slight bit dire.

The euro-skeptics, on the other hand, say nonsense, that the cost of leaving is slight and the benefits of independence and a secure immigration policy outweigh the pro-European position. They say the bureaucracy and budgetary costs (estimated at the equivalent of $500 million a week) of staying in Europe—are far too expensive.

The Common Agricultural Policy (CAP), the EU's most expensive policy, accounts for 40 percent of the EU budget— raising consumer prices by protecting inefficiency.

Euro-skeptics also calculate that the EU prevents the UK from other open trade, costing Britain about 4 percent of GDP to the economy. Further, for euro-skeptics, the euro zone crisis demonstrates what happens when ill-matched economies enter into a monetary union. Just look at Greece to see the type of severe consequences that are possible.

A year ago few people thought the Brits would actually leave Europe and were disappointed when it did not happen.

But today, after a rise in populism worldwide and growing nationalist sentiment, the UK decision to stay out of the Eurozone has a better chance to be prelude to a full-scale Brexit.

The idea that the Anglo-Saxons are Continentals has itself long been contested (since at least 1066), and European identity, let alone the flawed integrationist machinery of the Brussels experiment, is roundly questioned—well, perhaps detested might be closer to the prevailing view—especially as the Jean Monnet dream concept of "Europe" is being called into question in country after country.

The elite that that dominates EU decision-making is managerial, bureaucratic and socialist with a view to higher taxation and redistribution of wealth—all qualities the EU elite tout proudly, despite growing populist sentiment among an increasingly economically pressed middle class in virtually every EU-participating country.

Add to the mix the surge of Muslims fleeing the Middle East into Europe, and the strain on EU cohesion has reached a breaking point.

But from an American perspective should we care? Do we really have a dog in this fight?

London's mayor, the ever colorful Boris Johnson, who wants himself badly to be the next prime minister, said that the Obama position was "ridiculous "and that his views on the subject reflect a "part-Kenyan heritage"… "driving him toward anti-British sentiment."

Nigel Farge, the leader of the nationalist UK Independence Party (UKIP), went further and told Obama to "butt out."

The question US citizens should puzzle is this: Would you want the United States to join anything like the EU—a federal superstate that curtails sovereignty? Reread the definition provided above, and you decide.

Of course the answer is NO.

We wouldn't want that in any way, shape or form. And the British already, under Margaret Thatcher, decided not to become part of the flawed Euro currency and the European Central Bank. They have a kind of halfway house. In, but not all the way in. But the globalists that populate the EU, make no mistake, want a complete political union as the end game.

So here's an interesting and novel alternative no pundit is yet suggesting, and I say it only half facetiously.

If our "Very Special Relationship" partners (forgetting the War of Independence as a spat between cousins, as well as their torching of the White House in 1812) don't want to be Europeans (the island apart argument and Churchill's notion of the English speaking peoples)—why not give them *two* other viable alternative choices?

The United Kingdom could join the North American Free Trade Agreement (NAFTA), and we would rename it the North Atlantic Free Trade Agreement. Nothing to sneeze at and no costs attached, just a bigger free trade zone. No attendant superstate.

Or, more radically, and I jest not (well, maybe), give the U.K. statehood status and a proportional number of members of Congress, with two senators. That would make our relationship truly special. Why not throw in an NFL franchise for London? We like the queen, so she could have some honorific role. How about Queen of Queens?

British culture, food, and sport would *all* dramatically improve (at least from a US point of view), and together we would win all the Olympic medals.

Something to consider?

Seriously, we all should recall a profound speech given by then former Prime Minister Winston Churchill, in 1946, at Westminster College, in Fulton, Missouri.

It was perhaps his most significant post-war speech, where he launched both the phrases "iron curtain" and "special rela-tionship " into popular currency. He said our two countries shared a common history, a common language, and a common literature, observing that in the course of the twentieth century twice we had been on the same side in wars to defeat tyranny and dictatorship and for liberty and freedom.

Our mutual and abiding interests, common worldview, congruence of sympathies, and the undeniably unique heritage of the Anglo-American tradition of liberty is our true future together. With a shared Whig history, the King James Bible, the Anglican Church, long historical memory—all of these things make up a valuable Anglo-Atlanticist patrimony. Britain belongs here, with us in the United States, not part of an increasingly disunited Europe.

The twenty-first century will need such Anglo-American leadership more than ever before. Perhaps, herein lie the sinews of lasting peace.

TRUMP'S ANSWER TO ISLAMIC TERRORISTS

Donald Trump's campaign remarks about Muslims were both taken out of context and decoupled from a necessary, *larger* framework.

Trump is neither anti-Muslim nor against states with majority Muslim populations. Quite the opposite is in fact the case, as his long business associations, various joint ventures, and employment practices in the private sector prove. However, he is deadly serious, unlike the present administration, about protecting America from all terrorists. The unpleasant reality is that *most* of these terrorists come from the Muslim world. Why is that?

"Temporarily halting" migration and immigration of a group of people emanating from defined countries (especially undocumented refugees) is a safety precaution that would be put in place to put a stop to terrorism against Americans. That is the intended goal after events that could have been avoided. Presidents as diverse as FDR, Nixon, and Carter have initiated such practices in the past—so Trump is not out of bounds.

Trump's determination to re-examine US immigration policy in light of a realistic assessment of current terrorist threats should not be seen as a permanent measure. As Trump stated, we simply need to reinspect our current policies and procedures to insure that they are properly adapted to protect all Americans against the real threat posed by ISIS and other radical Islamist groups.

This process would be time sensitive and urgent. The goal would be to close loopholes and to put in place controls likely to work, including using social media to glean information on all visa applicants.

Without such measures, we only risk more terrorist activity on US soil. Both the CIA and the NSA have recently testified that such terrorist activity on American soil is likely. Should we not take precautions given the warnings authorities like the CIA and NSA have already issued?

The larger framework, however, should *not* be forgotten.

In 1996, the late, brilliant Harvard professor Samuel P. Huntington published a book entitled the *Clash of Civilizations* that was most prescient. Huntington suggested a theory that cultural and religious identities will be the primary source of conflict in the post-Cold War world.

It appears Huntington's analysis twenty years ago has today begun to come to fruition. His forecast becomes more relevant each passing day in our post-9/11 world, where the threat of Islamic radicalism is not only tearing at the social, economic and political fabric of America, Europe, Africa and Asia, but it also is the core conflict in a Middle East thrown into civil war by the centuries-old enmity still dividing Sunni and Shiite Muslims.

Global conflict today is increasingly about culture.

The battle lines of the present are not confined to the arc of the Muslim world spreading now into the United States, Europe, and Africa. The end of ideologically defined states in Eastern Europe and the Soviet Union has allowed traditional ethnic identities and animosities to rise; and rise they have. Just pause to ask how many different ethnic groups comprise the former Soviet Union, or take a moment to contemplate the hopes and dreams that motivate Kurds in nations like Iraq, Iran and Turkey to want their independence.

To quote Huntington himself: "The clash of civilizations thus occurs at two levels. At the micro-level, adjunct groups along the fault lines between civilizations of territory and with each other. At the macro-level, states from different civilizations compete with each other for relative military and economic power, struggle over the control of international institutions and third parties, and competitively promote their particular political and religious values."

The most significant dividing line in the world now is the Western boundary of Christianity in the year 1500. It is not only a divide but also a line of bloody conflict. That fault line between Western and Islamic civilizations has been going on for some thirteen hundred years. Islam twice laid siege to Vienna.

Huntington predicted that the interaction between the West and Islam would not decline but rather accelerate. He said it would become more violent. The historian Bernard Lewis came to the same conclusion; so did the distinguished Muslim scholar A. J. Akbar.

The larger conclusion for our debate today is that the West, especially led by the United States, will have to develop an understanding of various civilizations, primarily the violent aggression of radical Islam understood both as a religion and as a political movement. The United States today needs to maintain and rebuild the economic and military power necessary to protect our national interest, to better defend ourselves, protect our citizens, and preserve our civilization.

Trump understands that Islam is one of the three great Abrahamic faiths and that a minority of its adherents has hijacked Islam for violent political ends. Radical Islamic terrorists are destroying their own culture even as they strike out against everything they hate in Western civilization.

The truth is Islam needs to undergo the type of reformation

experienced by the other two Abrahamic faiths. Millions of Muslims throughout the world realize that the needed reformation must emanate from within Islam itself, such that it cannot be imposed on Islam from the outside.

For the needed reformation to take place, true-believing Muslims and Muslim-majority states must take back their own religion and oppose all forms radical Islam that profess political terrorism, with a resolve to condemn and defund Islamic terrorism wherever it raises its ugly head. This is the place to start.

Meanwhile, we need to both protect ourselves and combat terror with all the means at our disposal. This is not a half-hearted or feeble exercise. It will take time, money, and effort, and it starts with fixing our immigration system much as Trump has suggested, and by rereading Huntington to get a firm intellectual grasp on how best to resolve the global clash of civilizations that today threatens to destroy civilization itself.

SEVEN DAYS OF CREATION:

TRUMP'S FIRST WEEK AS PRESIDENT

Now that Trump has swept the electorate, what exactly will a Trump government do first? Imagine this creation narrative. In the Beginning . . .

On the **first day** the new president—in a year's time, after his swearing in—would do the three things he promised he would do *immediately:* end ALL of Obama's executive orders, stop Obamacare and institute Health Savings Accounts, and cut the head off of the snake called ISIS. In other words, from Day 1 we would have an acting president, again. His concrete plan to *defeat*, not just contain, the caliphate in Syria would be unleashed in a reign of power coordinated with many other willing partners. It will be called Operation Roaring Lion (borrowed from Hosea 11:10), and its objective will be a quick (one month) end to that plague.

Day 2 would see the complete emasculation of all the costly and nonsensical laws and regulations that impale Americans and their business opportunities. The day would also see a drop in the corporate tax rate to the lowest level in decades. Trump would then stop corporate inversion and bring back over a trillion dollars of American investment from overseas to be invested in new jobs here. Late in the day he would put a shovel in the earth, breaking ground for the new wall on our border with Mexico, to be paid for by a tax on Mexican oil. The wall will be technologically *impossible* to penetrate.

At bedtime he would change America's broken visa immigration program.

Day 3 Trump would start by endorsing the Second Amendment and ending gun control. Then he would roll out a comprehensive plan to *immediately* rebuild America's military. It will reflect the voice of the generals and admirals and reposition America for strength. Specifically, it will deliver the world's most formidable fighting force on the land, in the air, and on the sea. It will also put China, Russia, and North Korea on notice. All of America's international trade deals will be up for renegotiation, and burden-sharing will be effected with costs born by those countries we defend. The Iran deal would be rewritten in our interest, and Gitmo would be reopened.

On **Day 4** Trump would announce the Keystone pipeline and American energy self-sufficiency. He would change the US tax code and implement his tax reform plan. It would lower taxes for everyone and especially the needy and middle class. As a flatter tax, it would also end all the expensive gimmickry called tax planning and evasion. There would no deductions (except mortgages) and no loopholes. The corporate lobbyists would be out of a job. No one will need lawyers and accountants to do taxes any longer. The estate tax would also be repealed, at midnight.

Day 5 President Trump would announce a balanced budget and enact the line item veto. He will meet with the speaker of the House to say "we won't do business the same old way." All spending will progress in Congress as separate authorization bills, and there will be a *firm cap* on the debt ceiling. He will also announce a pledge, called "The George Washington Pledge," whereby every House member and senator will sign a contract *not* to run for more than two terms. Like our founding president, this will return America to a republic without an entrenched "political class" and will allow those in public elected service to literally return to their own Mount Vernons to pursue private lives, rather than decamp in the nation's capital for a lifetime. Anyone who refuses to sign it will be hounded out of office. And Trump will also announce that no elected or civil servant can ever lobby the government after leaving office—full stop. It would be made retroactive.

Day 6 will see the end of both the Department of Education and its Common Core, and the curtailment of the EPA. All funding for education will be reallocated to the states. This decentralization and empowerment of people, where they live, will be a continuing theme of Trump's administration as an act of *subsidiarity*. Private education will be funded at the same level as public education, and parents will be given the freedom of choice.

The country will be turned around in six days.

On the **seventh day**, as in the biblical Genesis story, after Trump bans late term abortion and defunds Planned Parenthood, the president and the nation will rest. The president will encourage all Americans, as is our tradition, to give thanks to God, ask for forgiveness, be generous and attend the religious institution (or none) of their choosing.

Then God blessed the seventh day and made it holy, because on it he rested from all the work of creating that he had done (Genesis 2:3).

America will be Great, again!

TRUMP'S WALL

THE PROBLEM

The US-Mexico border stretches for more than two thousand miles across very rugged terrain. It has become a symbol of insecurity and a complete failure of control. It has now become the *pivotal* political issue between the two countries and *the* hot-button issue in the 2016 US presidential election.

Why?

Simply because illegal Mexican (and other) undocumented aliens use it to traffic in drugs, guns, and persons.

Mexico is poor; the United States is rich. Economic opportunities encourage a near constant (over 20 million over the decades) flow of migrants into the United States. Terrorists can do the same. To date, it cannot be stopped.

About 12 million illegal immigrants now reside in the United States or 3.5 percent of our nation's population. Mexicans account for half of the unauthorized immigrants, according to a recent Pew survey. Most of the others come from Central America. Six states account for 60 percent of the illegals (CA, TX, FL, NY, NJ, IL). Nevada has the largest share at 8 percent of the unauthorized in its state population. About 27 percent of all K-12 students now have at least one unauthorized immigrant parent. The problem goes on and on, unabated.

As Donald Trump puts it, the problem is: A nation without borders is not a nation."

THE SOLUTION

A Star Wars, hi-tech electronic wall that uses satellites, mathematics, and drones to stop any and everything from crossing the US-Mexico border. Don't laugh!

It worked for Ronal Reagan and brought down the Soviet Union and it will work here. The technology exists and is getting better all the time.

This would be a new multifaceted approach to combat illegal immigration.

By using sophisticated analytical models, high resolution satellite imagery and loads and loads of big data (predictive analytics), applying proven algorithms, we *can now* predict where the flows will take place and deploy both border guards and laser (Taser) guns from armed drones to stun the perpetrators—thereby thwarting illegal entry of both people and drugs into the United States.

This is a *game changer*. Technology that will utilize aerial vehicles (UAVs) or drones, combined with other secret technology tools to reduce the flow across the border to close to zero.

Much of this technology is presently in use by the US military looking for the bad guys planting improvised explosive devices (IEDs) in Afghanistan and Iraq. The marvel of these technologies is that they provide an engineered solution where others have failed. The key is the satellites and the math, counting on the UAVs integrated into a *total solution package*. The UAVs are in effect our *eyes in the sky*. The live streams direct the drones and the rangers like chessmen on a board.

The illegals will not only be scared to death but they will also be instantly detected. They will no longer be able to operate with impunity. *Game over.*

PAYING FOR IT

Mexican citizens who work in the United States send billions of dollars back to Mexico every year. According to the World Bank the estimate of that amount exceeds $15 billion annually in remittances. The illegal Mexican workforce in the United States has increased by 125 percent in the last decade, which translates into lost jobs for Americans, large social costs, and unbearable burdens on our educational, health and welfare infrastructure in the communities and states where they poach off the US taxpayers.

Drug violence between the warring criminal cartels threatens security in Mexico and all the cities and towns along the entire border.

Tightening border security is not an option but a necessity.

The cost of this proposed high tech Wall is estimated to be $20 billion. As Trump has firmly stated, repeatedly on numerous occasions, "Mexico will pay for the Wall."

The question is how?

THE ANSWER

First, we impound all remittance payments to Mexico and Central America derived from illegal wages. Next, we increase all visa fees to all Mexicans. Third, we increase fees on all border crossing cards and worker visas from Mexico. Fourth, we impose a temporary and special tariff on Mexican goods at all ports of entry. And last, we commence a special tax of $30 per barrel on all Mexican oil and gas imported to the United States.

Guess what? Wall paid for.

Make no mistake: the United States must also coordinate the new hi-tech wall with other measures including: the immediate return of all criminal aliens, detention, not catch-and-release of all those apprehended in the future, closing down all sanctuary cities, enhancing penalties for overstaying on a visitor visa, pausing all new green-cards for foreign workers, ending birthright citizenship, and hiring many more Immigration and Customs Enforcement (ICE) employees to enforce our laws.

This is the way to solve the problem using a high tech total solution and having Mexico pay for it.

Don't say it can't be done: Let's do it, President Trump.

6

CONCLUSION

TRUMP'S COMMERCIAL REPUBLIC:
WHY AND HOW HE WON THE PRESIDENCY

In volume I, book XX of the *Spirit of the Laws,* Montesquieu provides the entire history of liberalism (with a small l as in limited government).

He is often cited as the source of the idea of checks and balances, or separation of powers, and thus as an intellectual inspiration of both the American founding and Enlightened European thought.

Among liberal advocates, Montesquieu is known above all for the notion of a *Commercial Republic*; namely, that trade between countries leads to peace among nation-states.

Let's begin by considering the mindset of Montesquieu by quoting the author of *Spirit of Laws* in book XX where he says,

Commerce is a cure for the most destructive prejudices; for it is almost a general rule, that wherever we find agreeable manners, there commerce flourishes; and that wherever there is commerce, there we meet with agreeable manners.

Let us not be astonished, then, if our manners are now less savage than formerly. Commerce has everywhere diffused a knowledge of the manners of all nations: these are compared one with another, and from this comparison arise the greatest advantages.

Commercial laws, it may be said, improve manners for the same reason that they destroy them. They corrupt the purest morals. This was the subject of Plato's complaints; and we every day see that they polish and refine the most barbarous.

OF THE SPIRIT OF COMMERCE

Peace is the natural effect of trade. Two nations who traffic with each other become reciprocally dependent; for if one has an interest in buying, the other has an interest in selling; and thus their union is founded on their mutual necessities.

But if the spirit of commerce unites nations, it does not in the same manner unite individuals. We see that in countries where the people move only by the spirit of commerce, they make a traffic of all the humane, all the moral virtues; the most trifling things, those which humanity would demand, are there done, or there given, only for money.

The spirit of trade produces in the mind of a man a certain sense of exact justice, opposite, on the one hand, to robbery, and on the other to those moral virtues, which forbid our always adhering rigidly to the rules of private interest, and suffer us to neglect this for the advantage of others.

The topic is the American election. The late night comedians are full of themselves over the results. One said, "there are two takeaways from last Tuesday: "Donald Trump got elected president and my job just got easier for the next four years."

He tried to find some consolation for Hillary Clinton supporters saying, "For the millions who are disappointed for Hillary, remember, America has a special place for people who lose. And ironically, it's the cast of *Celebrity Apprentice*."

For all the turmoil, turbulence, and sheer reality-show melodrama of the 2016 US presidential campaign, the actual results deepen long-standing trends in the electorate rather than shatter them. You may think the Trump election is a so-called *black swan* event or as one black commentator called it a 'white lash.'

It is not. Rather it is part and parcel of a much larger global pendulum swing towards populism and nationalism after decades of elitist globalism.

These trends are perceived as problematic for governance, partisanship, and democracy. But in fact they spell a different consequence, one that promises market-based solutions, more inclusive capitalism and greater participation and reassertion of national sovereignty.

I was asked to think about the title of this election and I couldn't help thinking it could be called "Creep or Crook," "Ultimate Insider vs. Ultimate Outsider," or perhaps, "Return of Batman to Gotham." That was the choice we faced—hardly entirely uplifting. "Vote for the one you dislike least" was often the rallying cry heard. But it didn't turn out that way.

The pundit class asked: Is this the best America, the land of the free and home of the brave could do? It perhaps begs the deeper question: Why is there such a dearth of leadership, nearly everywhere? It also shows how the Brexit wave times ten has now hit the US shores and in my analysis will reverberate back to Europe and then around the world.

That's been one of the paradoxes of this extraordinary election year. With both Donald Trump and Hillary Clinton facing unbelievably high unfavorable opinions from a vast majority of the voters, this has been a virtual "demolition derby of a campaign that has left both sides sputtering in the mud toward the finish line with dented fenders and cracked windshields." Yet a race that has unfolded like no other reinforces and intensifies many of the trends that have defined the competition for the White House over the past quarter-century. Yet all the experts, opinion makers, pollsters and elites got it wrong, badly wrong. Sound familiar?

It is hard to believe two years and about $8 billion dollars in total costs later this is where we are now. The American electorate has spoken or 55 percent of it, anyway. It is more a red country and Republicans control the House, Senate, and Presidency for the first time since 1928.

This gives Trump unprecedented powers—to undo the Obama legacy and by a combination of executive orders and Congressional logrolling to change America, to restore its pre-eminence militarily and economically, and simply put to lead again.

What are the major consequences for governing? Is the American Republic in peril, as so many leftist pundits here and elsewhere seem to fear? Should we move to a parliamentary democracy? Install proportional representation? Limit campaign spending? Have a six-week election cycle and drop all the crazy primaries. If only it were so simple! Not going to happen.

The polarizing nature of Trump's candidacy in particular pushed many of the dynamics that have shaped the electoral competition since the 1990s to new heights. They also empowered a large number of voters using emotional zeal and patriotism to unusual levels of enthusiasm.

With his brusque, even at times lewd message of defensive nationalism, Trump extended the GOP advantage in some places where it was already strong, both demographically (working-class whites and evangelical Christians) and geographically (non-metropolitan areas, Appalachian and Interior Plains states). But he also compounded the party's problems among other voters (college-educated and secular whites, minorities, and millennials) and in places (the nation's largest urban centers, coastal states) where the GOP was already facing crippling deficits. In particular, the distance between blue-collar white voters drawn to Trump with passionate intensity and both the college whites and minorities resisting him reached record heights.

Analyzing the data and exit polls, Trump actually did better with blacks, Latinos and woman than Romney, McCain, or Bush.

The cumulative effect leaves Republicans relying even heavily on the voters and regions that are most uneasy about the United States' cultural and significant demographic changes. Conversely, the election substantially subtracted from the Democratic advantage among the groups and regions more comfortable with those social changes.

This election widened every divide that fractures American politics—along lines of race, education, generation, and geography. American is a polity so fractured and divided it is difficult to civilly govern. Humpty Dumpty cannot be easily be put together again. The result is a coarsening of culture, an out of touch elite political class, a biased media and brokenness on nearly every front. The question and challenge is, as Trump himself vowed in his victory speech, "Now it's time for America to bind the wounds of division. . . . I say it is time for us to come together as one united people." "I pledge to every citizen of our land that I will be president for all Americans and this is so important to me."

The Trump victory means that Democrats may have barely won the popular vote in six of the past seven presidential elections, or since 1992 but the Republicans have a far superior strategic sensibility and know how to take the all-important Electoral College, which is after all how you win the Presidency.

This election is unprecedented and proves George Bush, hardly in jest, wrong —when he recanted that he may be the last Republican president.

Hello Donald, no thanks to the Bushes and the establishmentarians.

Trump's results however measure just how much separates a major portion of the electorate from the leadership class in virtually every American institution, ranging from business to the academy to national security to media, in the form of newspaper editorial boards—all of which coalesced in virtually unprecedented fashion *against* the tumultuous GOP nominee. Yet he won in spite of them!

A series of demographic and geographic factors determined the result we have just witnessed, while also sending critical signals about the future direction of American politics and democracy itself. Together, those underlying elements amount to tectonic plates that are shifting the United States. Only

Donald Trump foresaw those forces. The GOP did not; the experts did not and the candidacy of Hilary Clinton, so flawed by dishonesty and pay to play crookedness—was washed away even though she had a supposed insurmountable lead and all those celebrity endorsements.

One of the defining characteristics of American politics over the past generation has been what the sociologists call, "class inversion": the reversal of political allegiance among blue-and white-collar white voters. Through the first decades after World War II, every Democratic nominee from Adlai Stevenson through Jimmy Carter consistently ran better among white voters without a college education than whites that held advanced degrees.

But Republican gains, starting in the late 1960s, among whites without degrees and Democratic advances among college-educated whites, which accelerated in the 1990s, have reversed that pattern. Starting with Al Gore in 2000, every Democratic nominee has won a higher share of the vote among whites with a college degree than whites without advanced education. In his first victory in 2008, President Obama ran seven points better among college-educated than non-college-educated whites, the widest such gap ever for a Democratic nominee. Trump's appeal was to working class whites who have been left out; whose wages have stagnated; whose jobs have gone overseas; and whose kids live in the basement or face unemployment.

This campaign shattered everything and accelerates the class realignment of the two parties' coalitions. From the outset of his candidacy, Trump has established a visceral connection with many non-college-educated white voters, especially men. Competing in a seventeen-person field in the GOP primary, Trump still won nearly half of all non-college-educated Republicans; he led Clinton, usually by gaping margins, among that group in virtually every general post-election national survey.

Those voters turned out in record numbers for him, many so-called Reagan Democrats while minorities failed to get excited by the same old same old and a tired politician who had nothing new to offer other than sustaining the Obama legacy that failed to deliver the goods.

Republicans almost always now win working-class whites. The only Democrat to carry them since 1980 was Bill Clinton in 1992 and 1996, and he never attracted more than 44 percent of them. (That was enough for a slim plurality, though, because remember, many working-class whites supported Ross Perot's third-party candidacy.)

The real feat for Trump is how far he pushed the margin among these voters. In each election since 2000, exit polls show that the GOP nominee has carried non-college-educated white voters by at least 17 percentage points; Mitt Romney won them by 26 points, drawing 62 percent of them in 2012. Post- election polls show that Trump extended that advantage and even took Blue states like Ohio, Pennsylvania, and Michigan away from their Bluest status.

The ultimate mark of success for him was that he rivaled Ronald Reagan's dominant performance in 1984, when he won 66 percent of non-college-educated whites, beating Walter Mondale among those voters by 32 percentage points. But while Trump has made these inroads among working-class whites, he faced unprecedented resistance among whites holding at least a four-year college degree. Though Democratic nominees now routinely run better among whites with a degree than those without one, none of them have run well enough to actually win most college-educated whites.

In fact, no Democratic nominee in the history of modern polling, dating back to 1952, has ever won most whites holding a four-year degree or more, according to exit polls and the American National Election Studies. Hillary Clinton won among college-educated whites. Yet she lost the election.

And how did college-educated white men vote. Many of these ordinarily Republican-leaning voters—the GOP nominee has carried them by double digits in all but three elections since 1980—expressed skepticism toward both candidates, and polls varied widely on their preferences. It is now clear most of them drifted back toward their usual Republican inclinations, and in the end broke for Trump as did Independent voters. Trump fell well short of margins of twenty percentage points or more that these men have given the GOP nominee in three of the past four elections but he still carried the day.

These contrasting trends among college-educated and non-college-educated white voters produced a much wider gulf between the two groups than the record seven-point gap President Obama saw in 2008. Clinton ran fully twenty-two points better among college-educated whites—leading among them and drawing 47 percent support—than non-college-educated whites, where she drew under 25 percent support. All this points to a lasting new order in American electoral reality: realignment.

Two other trends in the class breakdown among whites are worth noting. One is regional variation. Democrats since 1992 have dominated the five key swing states in the Rustbelt—Ohio, Iowa, Michigan, Pennsylvania, and Wisconsin—largely because they have performed slightly better among these states' large populations of blue-collar whites than Democrats have among those voters nationally. Trump's results turned on whether he could end that advantage in enough states—and here he amazed everyone, as his numbers were unpredictably strong, his victory particularly resounding. It broke the Democrat hearts and will now cause an autopsy of strategy and tactics both

The results show two other things that auger well for the Republic— and for the Republicans. The first is, if Trump manages to keep America out of an immediate economic crisis, the long-run effects of his presidency will prove most profound. He could bring back economic growth, cut tax rates, create more jobs, and better distribute the economic benefits. However, the status of many international institutions is now in question. It is difficult to imagine new trade deals being completed, and old ones might be reopened or scrapped. President-elect Trump has some leeway to unilaterally impose temporary trade restrictions, and he will. He will also build a wall on the Mexican border and shift immigration policies.

And finally, as you may have guessed, for Europe: the prospects for concluding the Transatlantic Trade and Investment Partnership (TTIP) between the US and EU were already extremely poor, but in light of Trump's platform, the deal stands virtually no chance of being agreed.

In the UK, Brexiters can take heart from the victory of another anti-establishment figure. His political sympathies for Brexit could lead him to prioritize a trade agreement with the UK once the country leaves the EU. It will also insure a stronger US-UK Special Relationship.

Yes, Trump's success will embolden populist anti-establishment parties across Europe and around the world. Face it: this is the new reality but it is not necessarily injurious to democracy or to Montesquieu's original notions of a commercially based republic. In fact, it could under the best circumstances and, with the right personnel, enhance both.

TRUMP THE ARISTOTELIAN: WHY HE WON

Aristotle (384–322 BC), the Greek philosopher, founded communications theory some twenty-five hundred years ago and articulated it in his work on both politics and rhetoric. The two go together.

He said that persuasion comes from combining three elements in the right degree. Donald Trump has borrowed this magical elixir and is using it to get elected president. Trump is an Aristotelian—perhaps without knowing it.

What are those elements?

Any speaker (consider Trump on the stump) makes speeches on certain occasions (today in person, online, on television, and in print) to a given audience (targeted to location, theme, and group) in order to have effect (get votes to win an election or sell a bill of goods).

The process is *linear* and simple. The model in politics and business is speaker-centered. Trump has become expert at tailoring his comments to make a defined set of arguments to a very targeted audience and in a very specific situation. His objective has been to persuade. His rhetoric is emphatic. He has or is convincing the voters in Iowa, New Hampshire, South Carolina and soon the entire country that he, alone (well, with their help), can do one thing, namely: "make America great, again."

What is Trump's *Ethos*? In other words, what makes him credible? What is his "street cred," in the modern vernacular? You need this to establish a first line of communication, and that has to be *believable*. Trump's credibility is tied to his business acumen and success. It helps that he is universally recognizable as the chairman of the board on a popular TV reality show.

What is Trump's *Logos*? He is employing the means of *persuasion* by using logic, data and facts to get people to understand the situation we are facing as a country in decline and by saying he, as speaker and potential president, has a sense of reasonableness. How is he demonstrating that he knows what he is talking about and that he is in command of the present political and economic reality? He is doing that by stating figures on where we have gone down the wrong path and how that could be righted.

What is Trump's *Pathos*? His art of appealing to people's emotions is working. The emotional bond he deploys is captivating audiences as they feel connected both to him as leader and to his message. He is one of them. He gets their predicament. He is able to make voters see he can do something no one else can. Clearly, he is going to do things differently. He gets things done.

Have you heard of the 60-40 Rule?

It is simply this: You need 60 percent of your message to be *Pathos* to succeed. And for Trump that means he is emotively tapping into something the American public feels. They feel it because it surrounds them and angers them. The mainstream media and the majority of political leaders who have gamed the system to benefit themselves and the special interests that put them into power ignore it.

Here's what Trump comprehends that other politicians don't seem to get this year. Trump knows that to persuade is to influence someone by appealing to reason. But it gets you only so far. This is where emotion fits in. Trump is passionate, and his popular appeal to a future state of "greatness" is something

America and Americans once enjoyed and long to again.

The voters want to have economic growth, military resolve, cultural integrity, national sovereignty, and prosperity—again. It is both enlivening and powerfully optimistic. As Trump says, America is "crippled"—but doesn't have to stay that way. We did it to ourselves, and Washington, DC, is the reason why. Change the way Washington works and most all of Obama's policies, and we can revert to our past default path: greatness.

Trump knows that without stories you can't convince people. He knows this is why his own story is paramount. So, too, is that of all the entrepreneurs and all those who benefit in their wake. He utilizes theses stories to encourage people. The electorate has come to believe for the first time that *only* a businessperson, not some lawyer *cum* politician, can get us out of this mess and into a new cycle of American nirvana.

Logic alone doesn't work. Dale Carnegie said so in his many books on how to succeed. He was the premiere American pioneer in public speaking and personality development. He is perhaps the most well-known author in the field of communication and public speaking. Born in Maryville, Missouri, he grew up on a small farm and endured the struggles and poverty of rural life. He had a strong belief that the quickest way to develop a person's self-esteem was by public speaking. His book "How to Win Friends and Influence People" was published in 1930 and has now sold well over 10 million copies.

Carnegie truly believed in the saying, "Believe that you will succeed, and you will." He said, "There are four ways, and only four ways, in which we have contact with the world. We are evaluated and classified by these four contacts: what we do, how we look, what we say, and how we say it." Trump seems to have tapped the spirit of Carnegie and resonates his formulas. People like success. They like confidence and want to be with a winner. They also want a country that succeeds.

In recent times, brain scans have shown the same thing Carnegie intimated, only with more scientific backing than intuition. MRIs studying brain activity demonstrate that the brain lights up when a person feels success. Trump may be the *only* candidate who realizes this. He may be smarter than anyone else running—give him credit for that—and his "outsider" status in an election cycle that seeks to throw off the mantle of the insider "political class," no matter which party it represents, is also both good fortune and good timing.

But without *Ethos, Logos,* and especially *Pathos,* it wouldn't matter. Get those right and you win. Trump discovered the right formula and is on a roll. Only *hubris,* the dreaded Greek disease of ego, could take him down a notch. Showing some degree of humility may therefore be on order for The Donald as he moves past the general election.

EPILOGUE

TRUMP THE BUILDER

Until the election of Donald J. Trump as president of the United States this sentiment prevailed in most political and economic thinking: "Reflex internationalism needs to give way to responsible nationalism or else we will only see more distressing referendums and populist demagogues contending for high office."

Neoliberal allies can hold their noses all they like but the Brexit ball is bouncing. Like a *tsunami* it has washed ashore in the Trump victory and will soon reverberate back to Europe in coming elections in a raft of countries early next year. It will be felt as far away as India and China. Like the proverbial genie, it simply cannot be put back into the bottle—call it what you like. Brexit means Brexit and an end to globalist know betterism.

Make no mistake, Trump and his ilk are not anti-trade and most certainly, as entrepreneurs and most importantly *builders,* firmly believe in market-based fairly played capitalism. They just don't want or see the results of a long term system rigged to benefit only the few, the well connected, the super-elites, who game the system or force their one-world globalism on the rest of us.

Davos-man is dead.

Read the obituary. It is framed in the US election and all that Trump represents. The post-Berlin Wall globalization consensus is over. Going around telling the locals that they are racists for opposing migration does not help. They are not racists, they are nationalists—or better put "patriots" as H.G Wells called them in his prescient essay on the topic sixty odd years ago. The reality is that just like homeowners, these citizens of countries want to feel and see the benefits of home ownership or being a national.

Building the country is now Trump's political and economic imperative. Brexiters know the same sentiment and Mr. Farage was right all along. The government should use him as a back channel to Trump as they will need America in the next round of the "special relationship."

No longer des the world need to demean America, knock the dollar, have ultimate allegiance paid to corrupt international organizations and think that globalization or its attendant trade deals will solve all our ills. They won't. TPP (Trans-Pacific Partnership) is DOA (dead on arrival) and its European equivalent will be *next*.

In effect, globalism as an ideology and an economic process has also created a large number of discontents. It disenfranchised extensive swaths of our populations. Those groups have seen their median incomes fall in the last decade and a half and their costs rise, while disproportionally suffering from under and non-employment.

Thanks to blue-collar populism these working people have now spoken and they have found a voice in Trump, the Manhattan populist, who now represents them as president. But his Administration and what it will build is more about hope and change than rage.

Those fans of just about any government spending they can find, argue that only another not so shovel ready government bailout/financed infrastructure program can save the day. They would like to see the new Trump administration buy outdated ideas, borrow a ton of money and do a deal to have the public sector build back America. This crowd wants government to grow and control the economy—what was essentially the old Democrat model.

Trump will not buy that house.

Any Democrat proposed deal to have government build infrastructure is faulty from the get-go. It would be primed with political cronyism and paid for by the US taxpayer. It would incur yet more debt we don't need and can't afford and in the end accomplish *very* little—actually about the same as the original Obama-like plan achieved. And those results measured just slightly above zero.

Instead, here is the core of a program, revolving around the P in Public-Private Partnerships, namely: *Private Capital.*

This is an idea in formation that Trump is seriously toying with that could quite literally "make America great again," by rebuilding and renovating all US infrastructure and inner cities, its Interstate highways, bridges, tunnels, ports and airports. It could make them a beacon for others to envy and a statement on both technological prowess and private financing, while not using any government funding. This is a trillion-dollar plan—*all* of it from the private sector.

The concept involves returning to a private enterprise model to develop infrastructure. Companies like Verizon did not need a government subsidy or a government guarantee to build out a Wi-Fi Internet and a cellular telephone system nationwide. Why not? Because the profit potential of selling Internet and cellular services vastly outweighed the capital costs involved in constructing the next generation communication infrastructure.

Similarly, private capital is available for qualified infrastructure construction companies capable of building a wide variety of systems for the future—ranging from applying AI to the next generation of "smart superhighways" to designing energy generating power systems that utilize not only fossil fuel technology but also the next generation of solar and wind power. They can as well re-engineer and operate a wide range of services now considered strictly government provided, from charter schools, to prison systems of the future, to the possibility of revamping the nation's failing Veterans Administration into a voucher system incorporating private physicians and private hospitals.

Ever since Harvard's John Kenneth Galbraith published *The Affluent Society* in 1958, the political left in the United States and around the globe has been locked into the notion that "public goods and services" must be taxpayer funded and government operated.

Yet, even the federal government relies on a wide range of private contractors to provide needed military infrastructure worldwide, starting with government-approved contractors such as Bechtel, capable of building US bases of operation in far-ranging nations across the globe, to military contractors that design and build the nation's military hardware needed for the asymmetric warfare that is today and tomorrow's likely commonplace.

If infrastructure projects are economically viable, private insurance can be properly designed to provide bond-like guaranteed returns to institutional investors, including pension funds, mutual funds, and banks. They look for a certain return of principal plus a guaranteed rate of return over a specified period of time in order to lock in the type of no-risk investments required in the rigors of modern institutional investment portfolio design and management.

Consider that airports and toll roads of the very near future may be privately financed, privately built, and privately operated under government contracts that would require *no* taxpayer funding or guarantee, provided the operating contract offered the infrastructure construction and management company is designed to allow reasonable profits for a specified number of years into the future.

The McKinsey Institute and others have made the economic case that infrastructure investments pay off by expanding the economy and increasing the tax base. We all agree on that much. The real questions are: who pays, how much, and where?

Those like former Secretary of the Treasury Summers oppose this private sector thinking, unless it is packaged as a government initiative. He says, "It would be unfortunate if, in an effort to avoid deficits, large subsidies were given to private financial operators. Only when private-sector performance in building and operating infrastructure is likely to be better than what the public sector can do is there a compelling argument for privatization."

Nonsense. The voters have spoken and the last thing they

want is more government, costly fiscal policy, added bureaucracy, and old style cronyism for politicos and big city mayors
with their hands out. Remember that ultimately that money
comes out of the public purse.

Not this time; no thanks.

Like Bob the Builder of cartoon fame, Donald Trump must
now say, *"Can we fix it? Yes, we can."* And here's how.

AFTERWORD

BY NIGEL FARAGE

Just like Donald Trump's victory, the Brexit campaign is a movement against the establishment. Just as Brexiteers mobilized a people's army, so too has Mr. Trump mobilized the people in the United States.

Brexit is a story of a grassroots campaign, of putting on one's walking boots on, delivering leaflets, and going out to meet people in their communities.

The same way that Donald J. Trump mobilized people in the United States, we in the Brexit movement mobilized a people's army in the United Kingdom that went out and spoke to everybody and got them down to the polls.

In my words recently to the Brussels plutocracy, I suggested a much better future—one that is certainly shaped by what Donald Trump has sought in his resounding victory in the United Stares. Basically, I said:

> "Seventeen years ago I came here to the European Parliament
> and said that I wanted to lead a campaign to get Britain to

leave the European Union, you all laughed at me. Well, I have to say, you're not laughing now, are you?

"The reason you're so upset, the reason you're so angry, has been perfectly clear from all the angry exchanges. You, as a political project, are in denial.

You're in denial that your currency is failing. You're in denial . . . over Mrs. Merkel, or Mrs. Merkel's call last year for as many people as possible to cross the Mediterranean into the European Union has led to massive divisions between countries and within countries.

The biggest problem you've got, and the reason, the main reason the United Kingdom voted the way that it did is [because] you have by stealth and by deception—without ever telling the truth to the British, or the rest of the peoples of Europe— imposed on [the British people] a political union.

When the people in 2005 in the Netherlands and France voted against that political union, when they rejected the constitution, you simply ignored them and brought the Lisbon treaty in through the back door.

What happened [when the citizens of the United Kingdom voted to leave the EU] was a remarkable result, it was indeed a seismic result, not just for British politics, not for European politics, but perhaps even for global politics too.

What the ordinary people did, what the people who have been oppressed over the last few years and seen their living standards go down did, is they rejected the multinationals. They rejected the merchant banks, they rejected big politics, and they said, "Actually, we want our country back. We want our fishing waters back, and we want our borders back. We want to be an independent, self-governing, normal nation."

That is what we have done, and that is what must happen.

And in doing do we now offer a beacon of hope to democrats across the rest of the European continent. I make one prediction, the United Kingdom will not be the last member state to leave the European Union.

So what do we do next?

It's up to the British Government to invoke Article 50, and I have to say, that I don't think we should spend too long in doing it.

The British people have voted. We need to make sure it happens. [We need] a grown up and sensible attitude to how we negotiate a different relationship. Virtually none of you have ever done a proper job in your lives or worked in business or worked in trade or indeed ever created a job, but listen.

We used to protest against the establishment, and now the establishment protests against UKIP, so something has happened here. Let us listen to some simple pragmatic economics.

We, between us, between your countries and my country, we do an enormous amount of business in goods and services. That trade is mutually beneficial to both of us. That trade matters. If you were to decide to cut off your noses to spite your faces, and to reject any idea of a sensible trade deal, the consequences would be far worse for you than it would be for us, and I, even no deal is better for the United Kingdom than the current rotten deal that we've got.

But, if we were to move to a position where tariffs were re-introduced on products like motor cars, then hundreds of thousands of German workers would risk losing their jobs, so why don't we just be pragmatic, sensible, grown up, realistic, and let's cut between us a sensible tariff-free deal and thereafter, recognize that the United Kingdom will be your friend. That we will trade with you, we will cooperate with you, we will be your best friends in the world, but do that, do it sensibly and allow us to go off and pursue our global ambitions in the future.

Now we have an opportunity together, the United Sates and Great Britain in their long *special relationship,* to show the world how to do it—how to be free, again. How to be great, again.

It is Independence Day!

ABOUT THE AUTHOR

THEODORE ROOSEVELT MALLOCH is the author of a new memoir, *Davos, Aspen & Yale: My Life Behind the Elite Curtain as a Global Sherpa,* recently released by WND Books.

Malloch is Professor at Henley Business School and Senior Fellow at Oxford University. He served as Research Professor for the Spiritual Capital Initiative at Yale University. His most recent books concern the nature of virtuous enterprise, the practices of practical wisdom and "virtuous business," the pursuit of happiness, the virtue of generosity and the virtue of thrift. He is also Chairman and Chief Executive Officer of The Roosevelt Group, a leading strategic management and thought leadership company. He has served on the executive board of the World Economic Forum (DAVOS); has held an ambassadorial level position at the United Nations in Geneva, Switzerland; worked in the US State Department and Senate; did capital markets at Salomon Brothers on Wall Street, and has sat on a number of corporate, mutual fund, and not-for-profit boards, including the University of Toronto International Governing Council, a Pew Charitable Trust board, and the Templeton Foundation. Ted earned his Ph.D. in international political economy from the University of Toronto and took his B.A. from Gordon College and an M.Litt. from the University of Aberdeen on a St. Andrews Fellowship.

CREDITS

Many of the articles in this book were previously published and are reprinted with permission of the publisher. Those not listed here are original to this book.

"The New Roosevelt" on page 1 is courtesy of *Forbes*, http://www.forbes.com/sites/realspin/2015/12/15/donald-trump-teddy-roosevelt/#2c1922ec349c.

"The Manhattan Populist" on page 5 is courtesy of *Breitbart*, http://www.breitbart.com/2016-presidential-race/2016/05/25/the-manhattan-populist/.

"The Apprentice" on page 9 is Courtesy of WND, http://www.wnd.com/2016/05/the-apprentice-veep-edition/.

"For Not Against Trump" on page 13 is Courtesy of WND.

"How to Hire a CEO of These United States" on page 18 is Courtesy of WND, http://www.wnd.com/2016/06/how-to-hire-a-ceo-of-these-united-states/.

"The Noble Trump," on page 22, is Courtesy of WND, http://www.wnd.com/2016/05/the-noble-trump/.

"Commonsense Conservatism—From Reagan to Trump" on page 27 is Courtesy of WND, http://www.wnd.com/2016/03/common-sense-conservatism-from-reagan-to-trump/.

"Understanding Trump as a Principled Politician" on page 31 is Courtesy of WND, http://www.wnd.com/2016/03/understanding-trump-as-a-principled-politician/.

"Trump's Voice for the Voiceless: A New Majority" on page 36 is Courtesy of WND, http://www.wnd.com/2016/02/trumps-voice-for-the-voiceless-a-new-majority/.

"President Trump's Limited Government" on page 41 is Courtesy of WND, http://www.wnd.com/2016/02/president-trumps-limited-government/.

"The Candidate Who'll Restore US Spiritual Capital" on page 45 is Courtesy of WND, http://www.wnd.com/2016/01/the-candidate-wholl-restore-u-s-spiritual-capital/.

"Hillary Misery 2020" on page 50 is Courtesy of WND, http://www.wnd.com/2016/07/hillary-misery-2020/.

"America Is Home to Two World-Class Kleptocrats" on page 55 is Courtesy of WND, http://www.wnd.com/2016/07/america-is-home-to-2-world-class-kleptocrats/.

"'Pardon Me,'" Hillary Asks, 'until I Can Pardon Myself'" on page 61 is Courtesy of WND, http://www.wnd.com/2016/05/pardon-me-hillary-asks-until-i-can-pardon-myself/.

"Obama's Final 'Victory Tour': A Global Thugfest" on page 65 is Courtesy of WND, http://www.wnd.com/2016/03/obamas-final-victory-tour-a-global-thugfest/.

"Mirror, Mirror, on the Political Wall…" on page 69 is Courtesy of WND.

"Clinton: Too Big to Jail" on page 76 is Courtesy of WND.

"Krugman Nearly Always Wrong" on page 82 is courtesy of Breitbart, http://www.breitbart.com/2016-presidential-race/2016/06/14/paul-krugman-is-nearly-always-wrong/.

"The Rise of Nationalism Can No Longer Be Denied" on page 86 is Courtesy of WND, http://www.wnd.com/2016/06/the-rise-of-nationalism-can-no-longer-be-denied/.

"Revenge of the Literati" on page 91 is Courtesy of WND, http://www.wnd.com/2016/05/revenge-of-the-literati/.

"Who's Spewing 'Hate Speech'?" on page 95 is Courtesy of WND, http://www.wnd.com/2016/04/whos-spewing-hate-speech/.

"The Death of Europe" on page 100 is Courtesy of WND, http://www.wnd.com/2016/03/the-death-of-europe/.

"Why Religious Liberty Is Key to Prosperity" on page 105 is Courtesy of WND, http://www.wnd.com/2016/02/why-religious-liberty-is-key-to-prosperity/.

"Trump's Path to Fixing Trade" on page 118 is Courtesy of WND, http://www.wnd.com/2016/05/trumps-path-to-fixing-trade/.

"UN Skyscraper: Site for Trump's Newest Tower?" on page 123 is Courtesy of WND, http://www.wnd.com/2016/05/u-n-skyscraper-site-for-trumps-newest-tower/.

"A Better Option for UK: Become Our Fifty-First State" on page 127 is Courtesy of WND, http://www.wnd.com/2016/05/a-better-option-for-u-k-become-our-51st-state/.

"Trump's Answer to Islamic Terrorists" on page 132 is Courtesy of WND, http://www.wnd.com/2016/02/why-trumps-right-about-muslims/.

"Seven Days of Creation: Trump's First Week as President" on page 136 is Courtesy of WND, http://www.wnd.com/2016/01/7-days-of-creation-trumps-1st-week-as-president/.

"Trump's Wall" on page 140 is courtesy of *Breitbart*, http://www.breitbart.com/2016-presidential-race/2016/05/10/malloch-building-donald-trumps-border-wall/.

"Trump the Aristotelian: Why He's Won" on page 155 is Courtesy of WND, http://www.wnd.com/2016/02/trump-the-aristotelian-why-hes-winning/.